KORCZAK
Storyteller in Stone

Boston To Crazy Horse
September 6, 1908   October 20, 1982

by Robb DeV.

Published by
Korczak's Heritage, Inc.
Crazy Horse, S.D. 57730

FRONT COVER — Sculptor Korczak Ziolkowski pictured in the mid-1960's with his large 1/34 scale model for the Crazy Horse mountain carving, seen nearly one mile in the distance with approximately three million tons removed. As he continued blocking-out the colossal mountain carving in-the-round, Korczak had removed approximately 7.4-million tons at the time of his death, Oct. 20, 1982, at age 74. His wife, Ruth, and large family are dedicated to carrying on his work according to the detailed plans and measurements he prepared and left for that purpose.

BACK COVER — (Photo by Robb DeWall) Korczak inside the cab of his 72-ton D-9 Cat "Zeus," telling of the perils of bulldozing high above the treetops on the 563-foot-high Crazy Horse mountain carving, where he had many close calls over the years.

THE MONOGRAMS of Indian children at play which begin each section of this book were drawn by Marinka Ziolkowski, youngest daughter of Sculptor and Mrs. Korczak Ziolkowski.

Readers of this book may be interested in the following publications dealing with the life and work of Sculptor Korczak Ziolkowski. All are available **exclusively** at Crazy Horse Memorial or by mail order. Current prices or other information can be obtained by writing: CRAZY HORSE, Avenue of the Chiefs, The Black Hills, Crazy Horse, S.D. 57730-9998.

THE SAGA OF SITTING BULL'S BONES: The Unusual Story Behind Sculptor Korczak Ziolkowski's Memorial to Chief Sitting Bull by Robb DeWall. A 320-page hardback written as a novel, it deals — in part — with Korczak's philosophy of art and sculpture. Traces the controversial 1953 "theft" of Sitting Bull's remains from North Dakota and their reburial in South Dakota. Contains many historic photographs and newspaper reprints.

CRAZY HORSE and KORCZAK: The Story of an Epic Mountain Carving by Robb DeWall and illustrated by Marinka Ziolkowski. A 154-page hardback including photographs and 61 sketches by the youngest daughter of Sculptor and Mrs. Korczak Ziolkowski. Popular with readers of all ages although written primarily for young people of about junior high school age.

Crazy Horse Mountain Carving color booklet. A 26-page collection of color photographs showing the progress on the mountain carving from 1948 to the present. Also features Korczak's family and the Indian Museum of North America.

Mountain Progress accordion folder. Postcard-size collection of 16 color pictures showing the dramatic changes on the Crazy Horse mountain carving.

Sculpture Folder. A postcard-size collection of 14 color photos of selected marble sculpture by Korczak.

KORCZAK'S DREAM. A 16" x 20" color print on quality stock suitable for framing showing how Korczak's non-profit Crazy Horse humanitarian project will look when completed. Available rolled or matted. (A small black and white of this color print appears on pp. 78-79 of this book.)

KORCZAK: Storyteller in Stone
Copyright ©1984 by Korczak's Heritage, Inc.
Crazy Horse, S.D. 57730-9998

First Edition:
First printing, June 3, 1983

Second Revised Edition:
First printing, November 23, 1984
Second printing, June 26, 1986

Library of Congress Catalog Number: 84-52404

Mrs. Korczak Ziolkowski would like to thank the Reverend Joseph Swastek for his research contribution to this book.

The Making of a Sculptor

 hat an honor for a little Polish orphan boy from Boston to be asked by those old Indian Chiefs to tell the story of a race of people. What an honor! Only in America could a man carve a mountain.''

Sculptor Korczak Ziolkowski repeated those words many times during the 35 difficult years he labored on his Crazy Horse mountain carving, the largest sculptural undertaking the world has ever known. A proud American who shunned federal financing for his work, relying instead on the free enterprise system in which he believed so strongly, Korczak was both humbled and driven by that mission—to tell the story in stone of the American Indian.

Described by many as a premier sculptor of the age, Korczak was a self-taught sculptor, architect and engineer who never took one lesson in art or sculpture. Yet, he left a mark which will be felt by future generations because his enormous talent and vision created a unique humanitarian project which, by his own design, continues to progress and grow after his lifetime.

The Early Years

Korczak was born in Boston, the most Yankeeish of America's many thousand towns, the city of "pretensions, illusions, notions, tribal taboos and compulsions" maintained with sacrosanct rigidity by a plutocratic aristocracy which, in the words of an American social historian, is "as sharply differentiated a species as any nature has produced." Korczak was born on September 6, 1908, the son of Joseph and Anne Ziolkowski. Their untimely death in a tragic accident orphaned the lad at the age of one and severed his connections with the Polish background for many years.

After his parents' death the youngster lived a friendless, drudgery-laden life under the dubious care of an Irish guardian, who combined the somewhat disparate pursuits of a professional prize fighter and a professional builder. His wife was especially cruel to the boy. Korczak has characterized this phase of his growth to maturity as "a terrible life. . . . I was beaten and mistreated, and worked like a slave."

At the age of sixteen, Korczak left his heavy-handed guardian and started life on his own in a world that was not much more friendly nor more helpful than his taskmaster's had been. Hungering for knowledge and not afraid to work for it in and out of the classroom, he took a number of odd jobs to work his way through school — including pressing pants in a tailor shop, clerking in a five-and-ten-cent store, running a mimeographing machine in Harvard's Widener Library, and ushering in a movie house. He managed somehow to complete his schooling and to graduate from the Rindge Technical School in 1927, finding time to play football and perhaps even to dream about his future during this brief and busy scholastic career.

After graduation, as a 17-year-old youth, toughened by athletics and matured by the exigencies of self-support, Korczak took a job in the East Boston shipyards of the Bethlehem Steel Corporation, where he spent six years working progressively as a ship's carpenter, pattern-maker and woodcarver. During this time, he came to know much about wood, its hardness and softness under the pressure of the carving knife, its varied grain and shade.

The years in the shipyard influenced young Ziolkowski's future. One of his first assignments was to repair a twelve-foot ship's figurehead of an Aztec chieftain. He began devoting his spare time to woodcarving, producing beautifully carved furnishings at first and in time turning to more serious efforts. At age 18 he made a grandfather's clock from 55 hand-carved pieces of Santa Domingo mahogany, a six-foot eagle for a summer home, a set of carved chessmen the tallest of which was 18 inches high for a specially constructed chessboard, a large burnished candelabrum—these represented some of his earliest artistic attempts. The work won favor, bringing commissions and attracting influential friends, the most helpful of whom was Boston Judge Frederick Pickering Cabot who took Korczak under his patronage. He encouraged the struggling

AN AMERICAN OF POLISH DESCENT

As his name indicates, Korczak Ziolkowski was of Polish descent, two generations removed from his ancestral cradle in ancient Krakow, the proud seat of Poland's medieval royalty and nobility. His grandfather, Ignacy Ziolkowski, who came to America in the nineteenth century, brought the title of a count which his American-born descendants have eschewed. Nevertheless, a vestige of this aristocratic origin seems to have survived in the sculptor's first name, Korczak, which is particularly interesting for the fact that, while Polish in spelling and derivation, it is not strictly a personal name at all, much less a Christian name.

According to Samuel Linde's monumental dictionary of the Polish language $k\ o\ r\ c\ z\ a\ k$ is a heraldic term designating an escutcheon with a helmet, a hound's head and three bars. Another Polish philologist, Aleksander Bruckner, traces the etymological origin of the term to a common medieval Polish word meaning a wooden bowl or drinking cup. At one time, too, *korczak* meant a particular kind of windmill found in old Poland. Why Korczak received or adopted this unusual appellation in place of a Christian name has never been satisfactorily explained. Only the simple fact remains undeniable: Korczak Ziolkowski proudly bore a doubly Polish name to whose illustrious European lineage he added an American luster.

Korczak at age four

A sculptor at age 24

Beginning Crazy Horse at age 40

The mountain man at age 64

self-taught woodcarver, introduced him to prospective patrons, and, perhaps most important, acquainted him with Jan Kirchmayer who did the carvings for the Protestant Episcopal cathedral of St. John the Divine in New York City.

Young Ziolkowski attached much significance to this meeting with Kirchmayer whom he came to regard as "one of the greatest woodcarvers of all time," confessing in a newspaper interview some years after Kirchmayer's death, that he owed his final decision to adopt sculpture as a career to Kirchmayer. It seems, further, that Kirchmayer influenced Korczak in another way, by awakening and stimulating Korczak's awareness of his Polish origin and inspiring him with a desire to explore the riches of his Polish cultural heritage from which he had been cut off by the tragic and untimely death of his parents. Among Korczak's most cherished possessions were several mementos left him by Kirchmayer — some carving tools, a cashmere shawl, and an unfinished Station of the Cross.

Korczak's first sculpture was this life size plaster study of Michelangelo, which he created in 1928 at the age of 20. Although Korczak never took a lesson in sculpture or art, he educated himself in the fine arts by studying the Old Masters.

© KORCZAK, Sc.

When Judge Cabot died in 1932, Korczak was no longer a shipyard worker but a rising 24-year-old woodcarver of promise in Boston. He had not as yet tried his hand at carving stone, but Judge Cabot's death inspired him to purchase a block of marble and to carve Judge Cabot's likeness out of it. The remarkable head, carved from memory and without so much as a photograph to go by, was well received and in 1933 was placed permanently in the Judge Baker Guidance Center in Boston. Another distinguished Cabot Memorial, made three years later, is in Symphony Hall, Boston.

Encouraged by his initial effort, Korczak decided to devote most of his time to sculpture, choosing marble as his favorite medium. Some of his principal sculptural works produced after 1933 included the busts of Henry Noble MacCracken, president of Vassar College; Artur Schnabel, pianist and

Examples of Furniture Korczak Created and Carved

At 18 Korczak made this delicate 18" high chalice from 33 pieces of Santa Domingo mahogany. Intricately designed, it can be opened to reveal three "hidden" compartments.

© KORCZAK, Sc.

© KORCZAK, Sc.

One of the finest pieces of furniture Korczak carved is this six-foot-high chair featuring lions heads on the arms (with ivory teeth) and a high back topped with the Korczak family coat of arms. He also did the petit point and needle point on the back of the seat.

© KORCZAK, Sc.

This stained Georgia pine chess set was carved when Korczak was about 20. The king is 18" high, the pawns 8". He created it for an octagonal chess house in which a 12' square of the floor was the chessboard. He made 6'3" long forks for moving the chess pieces.

7

foremost exponent of Bach; Georges Enesco, the Rumanian composer and violinist; Wilbur Cross, former governor of Connecticut; Olga Alverino, the famous singer; and, the hands of composer-conductor Leopold Stokowski and the hands of the noted actress Katherine Cornell. His portrait of Ignacy Paderewski, the great Polish pianist and statesman, won first prize by popular vote at the New York World's Fair in 1939.

That same year Korczak accepted Gutzon Borglum's invitation to work as assistant sculptor on the famed Mount Rushmore National Memorial in the Black Hills of South Dakota. Both men were members of the National Sculpture Society and the famous Player's Club in New York City, so they had numerous mutual friends and many common interests. Although Borglum and Korczak got along very well, their association ended after only two and one-half months when Korczak got into a serious altercation with Borglum's son.

He returned to the East and in 1941-42 carved a 13½-foot-high figure of Noah Webster, the famed lexicographer, out of a single 33-ton block of Tennessee marble. The huge statue now stands imposingly on the Town Hall lawn of West Hartford, Connecticut, Webster's birthplace.

With the Second World War underway, Korczak volunteered for the Army in 1943, and was accepted in spite of the fact he was 34 years old. He landed on Omaha Beach, was seriously wounded twice, and rose to the rank of Sergeant, Chief of Section, in the anti-aircraft artillery.

During lulls in action, Korczak would carve with whatever might be at hand. From a downed tree he sculpted with an axe a striking eight-foot-high wooden bust of General Charles De Gaulle, now in the Museum at Rouen, France. Upon conclusion of the war, Korczak returned to civilian life and undertook a project that had been taking shape in his mind since 1939.

Late that year he had received a letter from an old Sioux Indian Chief, Henry Standing Bear, who lived on South Dakota's Pine Ridge Indian Reservation. He asked Korczak if he would be interested in carving a mountain memorial in the Black Hills to their great Chief Crazy Horse. Standing Bear wrote: "My fellow Chiefs and I would like the White Man to know the Red Man had great heroes, too."

After extensive study about the American Indian and several meetings with Standing Bear, the sculptor still was undecided about the proposal. At the time he was deeply involved with the Noah Webster Statue, which took two years of his life. Then, the next three years were claimed by the Second World War.

It was during this time of death and destruction that Korczak's desire to carve the Indian Memorial crystallized. After thinking it over for more than six years, he had decided to accept the Indians' invitation to come to the Black Hills to carve a mountain.

A keen student of history and philosophy, Korczak always referred to himself as a storyteller in stone. He believed one of the functions of sculpture could be to teach. He said, "I write (in stone) so those who run can read." An examination of how he came to create two of his most famous works, *Noah Webster* and *Paderewski,* illustrates that philosophy and helps explain his decision to devote the second half of his life to the colossal Crazy Horse mountain carving.

Study of an Immortal

mong the many outstanding statues that Korczak Ziolkowski carved out of marble and wood, none is more interesting in conception nor more striking in execution than the marble head of Ignacy Paderewski, world-famed Polish pianist-patriot. It stands three feet high and weighs 1,200 pounds. It was carved without the aid of a living model in 5½ inspired days. And, it carries the arresting inscription, *Study of an Immortal.*

Korczak Ziolkowski was twenty-seven years old, enjoying a small local reputation at West Hartford, Connecticut, as a promising self-taught woodcarver and sculptor, when he decided to carve the head of Paderewski. He had already done some fine work in wood and marble for private collectors and public institutions.

The years had also brought much hope and considerable progress — accidental interest in woodcarving, generous encouragement of influential friends, growing development of native artistic talent, special recognition at the age of twenty-five when Korczak sculptured his first important statue (a marble head of Judge Cabot), and marriage a year later into one of Connecticut's oldest families.

The precise reason why Korczak turned his attention to Paderewski whom he had never seen face to face remains a matter of conjecture, since the sculptor has not divulged it in any of his interviews with the press. Perhaps Korczak, a confirmed believer in tradition and heritage, sought to reestablish stronger cultural ties with his ancestral background by immortalizing in stone the features of one of Poland's great sons. Possibly he discovered some kinship between his maternal relatives and the family of Paderewski's first wife, Antonina Korczak. He might have read Charles Phillips' revealing biography, *Paderewski — The Story of a Modern Immortal,* and found in its interpretation of Paderewski's personality as "the story of power realized through self-discipline" not only an echo of his own struggles but also a challenging inspiration to creative achievement.

Korczak with his 1,200 pound Carrara marble portrait of Paderewski, which won the first prize for sculpture at the 1939 New York World's Fair.

In any case, whatever the reason that inspired the statue, the undertaking was a happy and fruitful one. Korczak obtained several photographs of Paderewski, bought a block of marble weighing more than half a ton, and began working with mallet and chisel in his garage workshop at West Hartford. After 5½ feverishly intensive days (he called them "26-hour days") of chipping and polishing, out of the 1,600-pound marble block emerged a head of amazing forcefulness and arresting expression: a crag-like face with dark brooding eyes overhung by heavy brows like massive precipices, its mustached mouth closed firmly over a determined jaw — the whole surmounted by a high noble brow and encased in a rich mane of hair.

"Here is the great pianist and statesman, the 'lion himself'. . . in all his significance," wrote critic Marian Murray appreciatively of the statue. "It is not, in every detail, an accurate portrait. The heavy brows are a bit too exaggerated. The nose has not quite the contours of Paderewski's. Yet this is the man — for all the world to recognize.''

No one acquainted with Paderewski's features has difficulty recognizing him in Korczak's remarkable *Study of an Immortal*. Perhaps the unsurrendering tenacity stamped upon the massive face at first glance makes a disconcerting impact, since the characteristic is seldom popularly associated with the personality of Paderewski. But a closer examination of the nobly carved features reveals the dominant heroic trait of Paderewski's many-faceted character and varied career, which Charles Phillips has aptly described as ''the story of two men . . . the story of an artist and the story of a statesman, the story of a genius of music and of a genius of statecraft.'' Which of the two came first is open to discussion. Saint-Saens once remarked, ''Paderewski is a genius who happens to play the piano,'' while Paderewski himself wrote on one occasion: ''The Fatherland before everything, art afterward.''

The Paderewski sculptured by Korczak Ziolkowski in the *Study of an Immortal* is the patriot-statesman rather than the composer-pianist. The spirit that slumbers beneath the crag-like face is not that of the poetic romanticist at whose magic touch streams of lyric melody cascaded from the piano down the concert halls of Europe, America and Australia to linger unforgettably in the memories of enraptured listeners. It is rather the brooding spirit of the resolute patriot who with unobscured vision sees freedom robed in glory and, in the teeth of overwhelming tyrannies, Moses-like, dedicates himself with unyielding firmness of purpose to lead his nation to its free destiny.

More profoundly perhaps than any other artist, Korczak has grasped and exposed with stark realism not only the dominant motive of Paderewski's life but also its attendant tragedy and sacrifice nobly and heroically offered on the altar of the fatherland. He has enshrined in age-surviving stone the spirit of Paderewski, the indomitable Pole, whose life may well be summed up in the poignant Polish saying: ''I am grown not out of salt nor out of the soil but out of that which pains me.''

This growth out of pain can be briefly told. Born in the Podolian borderland of Russian-held Poland in 1860, Ignacy Jan Paderewski watched with the frightened eyes of a three-year-old boy as Cossack troops led his father away to Siberia during the tragic rising of 1863 which failed to restore freedom to partitioned Poland. Seventeen years later, still not yet of age though already a graduate of the Warsaw Conservatory and a husband and father, Paderewski gazed with tear-filled widower's eyes upon the corpse of his wife who had died giving birth to a son. Then for twenty years Paderewski watched over his motherless boy, Alfred, who remained a helpless invalid unable to walk, dying finally of pneumonia while his father was away on a concert tour.

Shortly after the outbreak of the first world war in 1914, Paderewski began an intensive four-year campaign for the recovery of Poland's freedom seized from her by three rapacious neighbors more than a century earlier. Through Colonel Edward House he met President Woodrow Wilson who in January 1918 proclaimed in the thirteenth of his famous Fourteen Points that Poland must once again be free. Twelve months later, Paderewski became Prime Minister of Poland's new independent government and its chief representative at the Peace Conference of Versailles, where he did much to advance the Polish cause.

Yet in December 1919, "undermined surreptitiously and openly threatened" by political opponents in Poland, Paderewski resigned the premiership and went to live in Switzerland. In spite of bitter disappointment, he continued to work for the Polish cause unremittingly during the remaining twenty-two years of his life. According to one biographer, most of the ten million dollars Paderewski made, in forty years of travelling nearly half a million miles to give more than two thousand concerts, went for the Polish cause.

When the Nazis invaded Poland in September 1939, precipitating the Second World War, the seventy-nine-year-old Paderewski hurried to the aid of his native land as he had done in 1914. To the hour of his death, which came to him in his eighty-first year in New York, June 29, 1941, he refused to surrender his faith in Poland's final victory and freedom. To the very end of his long and eventful life he remained, like Conrad's *Lord Jim,* a man "of unobscured vision and tenacity of purpose."

By this time Korczak's *Study of an Immortal* was six years old and widely exhibited. It was displayed in the Steinway Gallery in New York City and acclaimed as "undoubtedly the most important and distinguished work which Korczak Ziolkowski has done." Shown at the New York World's Fair in 1939, the most elaborate exposition ever staged in America to that time, the Paderewski head won the first prize for sculpture by a popular vote of more than sixty thousand persons. Originally on view in the Contemporary American Art Pavillion, officials of the Polish pavillion asked that Korczak's head of Paderewski be exhibited in their pavillion, where it was lavishly displayed.

Today the statue stands in the gallery at Ziolkowski's studio-home in the Black Hills of South Dakota, where the *Study of an Immortal* is a constant inspiration to Americans and a lasting and revered tribute to an indomitable Pole.

In 1970 the portrait of Paderewski was among the eight marble portraits carved by Korczak that were vandalized by a person with a hammer. The noses were broken off and various degrees of destruction done with other blows to the features. It was an inexpressible loss to Korczak who said at the time "I feel as if someone had broken every bone in my body. They were like my children and represent years of my life's work." Expressions of sympathy came from all parts of the country and world. (Though an individual was charged in the case, the trial ended with a hung jury.) Korczak never again used the entryway to his studio-home, lined with the vandalized portraits.

Korczak's portrait of Paderewski, one of the world's greatest pianists, on display in the main window of the Steinway Piano Company in New York City. Created in just five and one half days, Paderewski was widely exhibited before it was voted the public's favorite at the 1939 New York World's Fair. Over 60,000 ballots were cast in the contest titled: "I may not know much about art, but I know what I like."

Hewer of a Lost American

his is the story of two Americans who lived and worked almost a century apart, but who both served their country and struggled for her ideals, each in his own way and time, in spite of misunderstanding and opposition. How both their names came to be linked with the Connecticut town of West Hartford is a saga of Americanism.

The first of these two Americans is a man for whom a strong case can be made as one of the most influential figures in the social history of the United States. A man of many interests, he was a linguist, lexicographer, educator, historian, economist, political theorist, Biblical scholar, climatologist, medical researcher, legislator and journalist, leaving in each field a noteworthy achievement. Besides writing incisively in support of the Federalist view during the critical years of the Confederation and the early Republic, he served the newly established United States of America in many cultural capacities, winning the proud title of the "Schoolmaster of America."

He influenced generations of American children with his blue-backed *American Spelling Book* published in 1783 which sold over fifteen million copies in his own lifetime and more than sixty million in a century, and with his popular grade school reader, *An American Selection of Lessons in Reading and Speaking,* which appeared in the first of many editions in 1787. He left an indelible impress on the speech of adult Americans with his monumental *American Dictionary of the English Language* first issued in 1828. He made his influence felt on public morals, thought and reading habits, by putting out the first American revised (Protestant) version of the Bible, by publishing and editing a magazine, a weekly and daily, and by bringing about the enactment of the earliest American copyright laws which have survived in essence to this day.

As a twenty-five-year-old schoolmaster, he had declared in 1783, two years after Yorktown had assured the colonies their independence, that "America must be as independent in literature as she is in politics," dedicating himself to the struggle for the literary independence of the United States from England. Intensely devoted to cultural Americanism, he championed a distinctively

14

American language, which would not only differ orthographically from the mother English tongue but also serve as "a band of national union . . . of a brave and independent people." He also advocated a distinctively American system of education, insisting that Americans should not be "indebted to Great Britain for books to teach our children the letters of the alphabet."

This man was Noah Webster. He was born in 1758 in a little red farmhouse at West Hartford, where he received his earliest schooling and later did his early schoolmastering. He died at New Haven in 1843, after a turbulent life of eighty-five eventful years, many of them occupied with overcoming difficulties raised against his views and works. His own birthplace banned him on one occasion for wine-bibbing and dancing, and neglected to memorialize him for nearly a century after his death.

The second of the two Americans in this story bears the interesting and revealing name of Korczak Ziolkowski, who was born in Boston, Mass., sixty-five years after the death of Noah Webster.

By 1937 Korczak Ziolkowski established himself as one of New England's promising sculptors by dint of persevering, self-taught effort. Heads and hands of famous persons were immortalized in marble in the workshop at West Hartford, where Korczak made his home in 1935.

Korczak liked West Hartford. In its crisp atmosphere of Colonial heritage and earthy Americanism, he did some of his best work. The town not only brought him success but also appealed to his artistic sensibilities. As a sculptor who valued significance above decorative features in his work, Korczak discovered in the town's past a tradition of idealism which he determined to memorialize in marble, as his grateful tribute to the city's past and a hopeful contribution to its future. He found the embodiment of this idealism in West Hartford's most famous but artistically neglected son, Noah Webster, the champion of cultural Americanism. The idea of carving Webster's statue came to Korczak one day, while he was visiting Webster's birthplace in West Hartford and learned of the lack of a memorial to the town's greatest, and all but lost, American.

In October 1940, as the Second World War raged in Europe and Africa and as American boys began registering for the draft, Korczak proposed his idea to a group of prominent West Hartford citizens. He explained that if the town would meet the material expenses of the memorial, which he estimated at $16,500 (or about 43 cents per citizen), he would contribute his time and talent as a gift to the community. The project was approved and a committee was formed to raise the necessary funds by voluntary subscription. The local press and the town council applauded the plan and its initiator. The council donated a plot of ground in front of the town hall, approved the sculptor's model of the statue, and told him to go ahead with his idea.

The project got off to an excellent start. But after several months, something began to go wrong, perhaps under the growing tension of the war in Europe. The fund raising campaign started to lag after collecting $3,700 (about nine cents per citizen). Interest in the Webster memorial declined, and suggestions arose to drop the project and either return the money to the donors or turn it over to some more practical purpose. In spite of the growing coolness toward

Korczak had to improvise a huge flatbed trailer to transport the 33-ton block of marble.

The sculptor dug the deep hole for the foundation and mixed and poured the cement for the base of the heavy statue.

NOAH WEBSTER
STATUE
A Gift to the Town by the Sculptor
KORCZAK ZIOLKOWSKI
with the aid of the Community
EXPENSES   CONTRIBUTIONS

THIS IS A COMMUNITY PROJECT

Standing the rectangular 33-ton block of marble in place was an enormous task. To do it, Korczak built this heavy scaffold and chain falls. He learned such engineering skills from working construction as a boy and, later, working on the Boston waterfront.

the proposal, Korczak decided to go on with the memorial, after changing his original model of the statue, choosing less expensive marble, and eliminating all outside labor costs.

In May 1941 Korczak himself dug the foundation and poured the cement for the base of the statue. Then he watched Gov. J. Hurley officially initiate the memorial by digging a spadeful of soil in presence of the town council. Early in June, he ferried a 33-ton block of Tennessee marble in a specially improvised trailer from the freight yards across the city to the Town Hall plot, where he set it in place and began carving. The first thing he did was to cut about a foot off the top of the tall block of marble so the statue would not be taller than Michelangelo's *David*. He worked ten and twelve hours a day with an air drill and hand tools that eventually produced 11 tons of marble chips. From the

Korczak and the 33 ton, 14½-foot-tall block of Tennessee marble from which he carved the Noah Webster Statue.

17

Korczak often worked around the clock during the short summer seasons.

celebration on the Town Hall lawn.

Because of Noah Webster's association with ancient fife and drum music, Korczak invited the famous Mattatuck Drum Band to play for the ceremony. Webster had played the fife at Cambridge, Mass., when George Washington took command of the Continental Army during the American Revolution. Korczak later organized and played drum in the Noah Webster Fife and Drum Corps, which performed in many New England communities and once marched in a parade up New York's Fifth Avenue.

A special pageant for the occasion was created, taking the theme from those writings of Webster which spoke of his troubles and sacrifices. The celebration was climaxed by the formal dedication of the unfinished,

larger pieces of the marble removed from the shoulder cuts, Korczak carved his *Polish Eagle, Wilfred Funk* and the original *Crazy Horse* scale model.

Enthusiasm for the memorial began to revive, but chiefly among the students of West Hartford. Grade and high school pupils began a new house-to-house fund campaign that netted several hundred dollars. They worked at polishing the statue and clearing the chips. They sold marble souvenirs to interested visitors. They wrote essays about Webster and the memorial, which they came to regard as their particular possession. Their interest and enthusiasm spurred the sculptor on to additional sacrifices in the form of $7,000 of his own money, which he contributed to the memorial.

By October 1941, the statue was half-finished. To commemorate the 183rd anniversary of Noah Webster's birth, Korczak decided to hold a

Ruth Ross was one of the many students who volunteered to help Korczak with the statue. They married in 1950.

Korczak working on the Noah Webster head, which he recarved more than 30 times, perfecting its appearance under varying light conditions and from many different angles and distances.

22-ton, 13½-foot statue with its pointed inscription:

> For you I labored
>   not for my own day.
> That by the Word
>   men should know brotherhood.
> My fellow men!
>   you have not understood,
> Since each of you
>   would go his separate way.

Beneath this provocative inscription was a dedication which also pointedly read:

> As beautiful as giving is,
>   with grace,
> So have the few shared
> This eternal stone with all.
>   And Youth—
> Be it forever known—
> United past with Future
>   in this place.

The celebration brought into the open much of the pent-up sentiment that had been mounting in West Hartford since Korczak began work on the memorial in spite of the lack of wholehearted support. An observer described the resultant controversy as ''one of the most amazing stories in art, a story which transcends the furor made about MacMonnies' *Civil Virtue* set up in

City Hall park in New York which citizens repudiated, or Epstein's paintings in London, similarly repudiated by laymen of the British capital." Another reporter called it "one of the greatest popular controversies ever to arouse traditionally placid West Hartford."

Some of the 500 townspeople who witnessed the dedication ceremony saw in the pageant, in which Korczak played the role of aggrieved Webster defending himself against unjustified attacks, certain references to themselves. Others resented the participation of students who, dressed as Halloween witches, shrieked imprecations and heaped ridicule upon Webster's dictionary, using remarks which some listeners interpreted as mock comments upon statements made locally about the statue. The Hartford papers branded the pageant as an attempt of the sculptor to vent his grievances and disappointment in public. Other townspeople thought they saw in the inscription on the statue the ironic gesture of a chagrined artist — a slight to nonappreciative adults and a tribute to cooperative and understanding youngsters.

The authentically attired Noah Webster Fife and Drum Corps performed in many New England communities and on Fifth Avenue in New York City. Korczak is at left.

Korczak denied authorship of the first half of the inscription, saying the words came from one of Webster's unpublished letters written to John Jay in May, 1813. But the *Springfield Daily Republican* reported him as admitting that the words had been chosen because they aimed at the townspeople. It also quoted Korczak as charging that some prominent citizens had "repudiated" the orginal project and "refused to cooperate in the enterprise," and that, in consequence, the ideals of Noah Webster — brotherhood and democratic unity — had been "obliterated in the hearts of his fellow citizens."

Within a fortnight, half of West Hartford was up in arms. A petition was circulated to compel Korczak to efface the inscription. A move was started to denounce him officially in the town council meeting. Various charges, old and new, were hurled at the sculptor. He was described in such terms as "arrogant,

The completed <u>Noah Webster Statue</u> stands 13½ feet tall and weighs 22 tons. Popularly known as the "Schoolmaster to America," Webster is wearing his academic robes.

21

temperamental, and thinks he is the original genius.'' He was denounced for working on the statue on Sundays, for refusing to permit the transfer of the memorial to the Hall High School, and for giving the statue too small a head and "a rather short neck." There were rumors, also, that the statue would be defaced with red paint or even dynamited.

One local observer, Anne Whelan, called the opposition to Korczak "insidious and personal," stating that the sculptor played "the gratuitous role of hero and villain in one of those New England travesties which . . . savors of Salem witchcraftry." Another commentator, speaking of the "civil war of insults" that raged around Korczak's tribute to Webster, called the erection of the memorial "an epic of American life." Kurt Unkelbach, local radio writer, said: "West Hartford will always remember the year 1941 as the year when the school kids turned an ideal into a crusade."

Outside newspapers and magazines picked up the story and gave it national currency. *Time, Pic, The Architectural Forum,* and *The American Society Legion of Honor Magazine* ran accounts of the memorial which were generally favorable in tone to Korczak. So did the New York *Herald Tribune* under a headline that read: "Noah Webster's Home Town Cools to His Statue."

Perhaps the most interesting comment came from Buffalo's Polish daily, *Dziennik dla Wszystkich,* which saw in the West Hartford controversy unpleasant overtones and implications. It wrote editorially: "A group of so-called 'Yankees' is opposing our artist simply because he has dared to sculpture a statue of the great American educator, Noah Webster, which, in their view, should be carved only by a native American. In addition, they are most exasperated at Mr. Ziolkowski's name which they cannot pronounce at all."

Unembittered by the stir the memorial had raised, Korczak irrepressibly continued to carve the statue in full view of West Harford's passing citizens whose feeling gradually changed to resigned acceptance of the memorial. In the summer months of his second year's work on the statue, Korczak mowed 700 lawns to raise funds for the purchase of ten tons of cement needed to lay a sidewalk around the base of the memorial. Finally, after two years of unremitting and unrequited labor, heartbreak and personal expense, Korczak fully resurrected Noah Webster from the 33-ton block of marble, and presented West Hartford with perhaps the most unique statue in America, and certainly the largest statue hewn from a single marble monolith since Michelangelo carved his monumental *David* nearly 450 years ago.

Today, with the controversy largely a thing of the past, West Hartford's long unmemorialized most famous son stands majestically on the Town Hall lawn, gazing thoughtfully upon the passing Hartfordites many of whom, like millions of Americans throughout the country, carry the influence of his pioneer and far-sighted labors. And perhaps the thought that pleases most his marble mind as he looks out upon West Hartford and America, for whose ideals and unity he struggled in life, is this: that he owes his existence to an American of transplanted European parentage, who had such a profound understanding of the sacrifices that go to make a true American.

Thunder In The Sky

orczak arrived in the Black Hills to begin Crazy Horse Memorial on May 3, 1947. After a long search, he and Chief Henry Standing Bear had picked out the 600-foot-high mountain a year earlier, after Korczak was released from the Army. It had no name, so Korczak called it Thunderhead Mountain because of the unusual cloud formations over the mountain. He originally obtained it by purchasing — with his own money — a mining claim on the mountain.

Anyone could file a mining claim in the Black Hills and, in effect, "own" the land in question as long as $100 worth of assessment work was performed every year. Korczak found it ironic the government didn't care if the mountain ended up looking like an Indian on horseback, just as long as he did the required amount of assessment work each year.*

The sculptor had not wanted to locate the Indian Memorial in the Black Hills because of the proximity to Mt. Rushmore, on which Gutzon Borglum had carved the Shrine of Democracy. Additionally, he felt superior rock could be found elsewhere, perhaps in the Grand Tetons of Wyoming. But, the old Indians insisted the Memorial be in the Black Hills, which are sacred to the Indians.

Paha Sapa

The Black Hills are a small group of mountains partly in northeastern Wyoming but principally in western South Dakota. They stretch over a total area of about 6,000 square miles — roughly 100 miles in length and fifty miles in width — about a third of which is covered with dense dark pine from which the

---

*A photographic account of the progress at Crazy Horse is contained in a companion booklet, *CRAZY HORSE MEMORIAL, Carving a Dream* by Robb DeWall. Its 40 pages of color photographs feature the work and stages of progress on the mountain carving, the Indian Museum of North America, Korczak's studio-home and the Ziolkowski family. The 9"x12" photo album is available exclusively at Crazy Horse.

region derives its name. Fed by numerous streams and creeks, the region forms an oasis in a semi-arid plain.

This is one reason why the Dakota Indians, better known as the Sioux, came to the Black Hills more than a century ago. The Dakotas were the largest native group among the Sioux Indians. They numbered over 30,000 men, women and children and, according to an authority, were "universally conceded to be of the highest type, physically, mentally, and probably morally of any of the western tribes." Brave, vigorous, hardy and unrivalled as horsemen, they were described by one American general as "the best light cavalry in the world."

The Dakotas loved the Black Hills, which they called Paha Sapa, and regarded them with religious veneration as well as native affection and loyalty. They never lived in the Hills, but came only to pray, get tipi poles and hunt buffalo. Perhaps they knew of the incredibly rich mineral deposits of gold, silver, copper and tin hidden in the Black Hills — particularly gold. If they did, they made little noise about them and still less use of them, preferring the animal treasures found in the streams and woods. In this they differed from the white men who visited their hills from time to time.

In 1874, an expedition under General George Custer discovered gold in the Black Hills, starting the last important gold rush in the United States. The floating white population of the West — prospectors, miners, desperados — rushed into the hill oasis, peopling Deadwood and other mining towns almost overnight. Wild Bill Hickok, Calamity Jane and the Wells Fargo stagecoach drivers became familiar and fabulous figures in this "Richest One Hundred Miles Square in the World" — an area that fully justified its flamboyantly boastful designation by yielding over $100,000,000 in gold alone and becoming one of the richest gold-mining districts in the United States and the world.

It also became one of the bloodiest for a brief span of years. As the miners poured into the Black Hills, disrupting the primitive life of the natives and despoiling both people and land, the Sioux Indians rose to defend their sacred mountains and their fields and streams. Under the leadership of Sitting Bull and Crazy Horse, they overwhelmed the regiment of General Custer at the Little Big Horn in Montana in 1876 and temporarily stemmed the white man's invasion of their domain. But when they heard and faced the thunder of booming cannons, they soon realized that they fought a losing battle. Their arrows and anger were no match for the white man's artillery, artifice and ever increasing numbers.

Crazy Horse was bayoneted to death by a soldier at Fort Robinson, Nebraska, where Crazy Horse had gone under a flag of truce. According to several sources, he died in the early morning hours of September 6, 1877, at the age of only 33 or 34. One of the American officers who fought against him remarked upon his death: "Crazy Horse was one of the great soldiers of his day and generation. As the grave of Custer marked the high-water mark of Sioux supremacy in the trans-Mississippi region, so the grave of Crazy Horse marked the ebb."

The Sioux never recovered the blow, losing the Black Hills, as they had lost so much of their land elsewhere in America, to the white invaders who were ruthlessly pushing westward, driven by insatiable land hunger and greed for wealth. Dispossessed, exploited, beaten but never broken, the proud Sioux

Korczak and Chief Henry Standing Bear, who invited the sculptor to the Black Hills to carve an Indian Memorial. He wrote, "My fellow Chiefs and I would like the White Man to know the Red Man had great heroes, too."

treasured the memory of Chief Crazy Horse as a tragic symbol of the red man's greatness — a warrior martyred for his devotion to his race and land.

The Sculptural Design

It was the Indians who picked Crazy Horse for the mountain carving. In essence Crazy Horse was an Indian's Indian — an extraordinarily brave warrior and a brilliant military tactician, the first Indian known to have used the decoy system. He never surrendered, never signed a treaty and never went on the reservation. Also, he never allowed his picture to be taken. To white photographers wanting to take his picture, he scoffed, "Would you imprison my shadow, too?"

The Indian's reverence for Crazy Horse was a large factor in Korczak's dynamic sculptural design for the mountain carving—the titanic figure of the Indian Chief astride his stallion, pointing confidently with outstreched arm over the horse's head. Korczak wanted the mountain carving (and the Memorial) to reflect the pride of the American Indian, and he created its design after hearing the following story from the old Indian Chiefs.

They told him about Crazy Horse's encounter on the plains with a white trader who spoke Lakota, the Sioux language. This was after the Battle of Little Big Horn when most of the Sioux Indians had gone on the reservations. The white trader mocked Crazy Horse, who had refused to go on the reservation, and he taunted the Indian by asking him, "Where are your lands now?" Crazy Horse looked to the horizon, pointed over his horse's head, and proclaimed proudly, "My lands are where my dead lie buried."

Korczak's original 1/300 model for Crazy Horse is carved from Tennessee marble taken from a shoulder cut for the <u>Noah Webster Statue</u>. Crazy Horse is proclaiming, "My lands are where my dead lie buried."

The story being told on the mountain, "My lands are where my dead lie buried," is the story of the American Indian in the peak of his civilization — not in defeat, at the end of the trail. And, Crazy Horse Memorial is representative of all American Indians, not just the Sioux. Korczak wanted to tell about the race of people who inhabited the North American continent 400 centuries before the coming of the white man. He wanted to tell the world about the amazing culture of the American Indian and of his willing gifts to the white man of potatoes, corn, squash, tobacco, beans and some of the world's major products. Thus, as with *Noah Webster, Paderewski* and many other of Korczak's works of sculpture, Crazy Horse, in part, is invoking history.

A Humanitarian Project

During the six years that elapsed between Standing Bear's first letter and Korczak's decision to accept the Indians' invitation to carve their Memorial, the sculptor had determined the project would be much more than a mountain carving. He did not want Crazy Horse ever to be a "tourist gimmick," but a Memorial to benefit the Indian people culturally and educationally.

In the six years he thought about the invitation, Korczak reached the conclusion Crazy Horse must be a non-profit humanitarian undertaking. It would have three major goals: the mountain carving, the Indian Museum of North America and the University and Medical Training Center for the North American Indian. And, soon after his arrival in the Black Hills, he drew up a detailed master plan for the Memorial incorporating those three goals.

Korczak's vision for Crazy Horse was for it to be a link joining the past with the present and bridging the gap between the present and the future. It would preserve the ancient Indian arts and ceremonial customs as the Indian's contribution to the multi-colored culture of America. It would serve as the world's foremost Indian treasure house of culture where all red Americans might work for the expansion and deepening of Indian life in America—where the red American might meet the white American proudly and honorably.

It was on this basis that the Federal Government granted the Crazy Horse Memorial Foundation non-profit status in 1949. An impressive group of Americans was named to serve as the Foundation's board of directors, which continues to oversee the non-profit project today.

In the early 1950's, a land exchange was completed with the Federal Government wherein the Crazy Horse Foundation acquired 328 acres around the mountain and in 1982 a second exchange was completed which totalled 369 acres comprising 19 small isolated parcels of land surrounded on either three or four sides by land already owned by the Foundation.

Korczak felt it was "ironic that the Crazy Horse Foundation had to buy land from the state of South Dakota to give to the Federal Government in exchange for the land the government owned at Crazy Horse in order that the Crazy Horse Memorial could be carved — and could grow for the benefit of the Indian people from whom we took the land in the first place."

The Humble Beginning

Korczak's first two years at Crazy Horse were consumed pioneering in a

Why the Indians Chose Crazy Horse for the Mountain Carving

Crazy Horse was born on Rapid Creek about 40 miles northeast of Thunderhead Mt. in the year 1843 (?).

He was killed at Fort Robinson by an American soldier on September 6, 1877, while under a flag of truce — age 34.

Crazy Horse defended his people and their way of life in the only manner he knew.

BUT —

Only after he saw the Treaty of 1868 broken. This treaty, signed by the President of the United States, said, "as long as rivers run and grass grows and trees bear leaves, Paha Sapa, — the Black Hills of Dakota — will forever be the sacred land of the Sioux Indians."

Only after he saw his leader, Conquering Bear, exterminated by treachery.

Only after he saw the failure of the government agents to bring required treaty guarantees, such as meat, clothing, tents and necessities for existence which they were to receive for having given up their lands and gone to live on the reservations.

Only after he saw his peoples' lives and their way of life ravaged and destroyed.

Crazy Horse has never been known to have signed a treaty or touched the pen.

Crazy Horse, as far as the scale model is concerned, is to be carved not so much as a lineal likeness, but more as a memorial to the spirit of Crazy Horse — to his people. With his left hand thrown out pointing in answer to the derisive question asked by a white man, "Where are your lands now?" he replied, "My lands are where my dead lie buried."

May 29, 1949
Korczak Ziolkowski, Sc.

virtual wilderness. When he arrived at Crazy Horse there were no roads, water or electricity. He lived in an Army tent the first seven months while carving out a place to live. He felled trees and hand built the original log studio-home. The unusual structure has log beams 70 feet long and a roof that includes a 30-foot skylight.

Anxious to provide an attractive and interesting place for visitors, he filled the studio-home with his extensive collection of antiques and many of his works of sculpture. A number of Korczak's marble portraits including *Paderewski* were placed outside along the entrance walkway. And, each year during the winter months he added a couple of rooms to the visitor complex, which now totals more than 61 rooms built by Korczak.

Although he had come West to carve a mountain, virtually all of 1947 and 1948 were spent "pioneering," making a place to live and for the visitors while getting ready to start the mountain. That included clearing timber to build the first long road to the studio and then on to the mountain.

Not only did the first two years of intense building activity consume a great amount of Korczak's energy, it also depleted his modest resources. By the time he was ready to start the mountain carving in 1949 he had only $174 left to his name. He also was 40 years old and virtually starting his life over.

Dedication Of The Mountain

The Crazy Horse mountain carving officially was dedicated on June 3, 1948. Chief Standing Bear touched off a dynamite charge that thundered across the skies and blasted the first 10 tons of rock off Thunderhead Mountain.

Contemporary chronicles of this first blast described it as an event "of significance to the American Indian." They spoke glowingly of the colorful ceremony accompanying the official dedication and initiation of the project by which "for the first time in history the red Americans are being honored by white Americans." Among the four hundred bedecked Indians who took part in the ceremony were five of the nine remaining survivors of the Battle of the Little Big Horn.

The five survivors of Little Big Horn were very enthusiastic about the planned Memorial, particularly the humanitarian aspects. Through translators they also told Korczak many stories about Crazy Horse, telling about his unusual qualities and describing what he looked like in great detail. They also confirmed that Crazy Horse had worn a stone at his ear and, when asked about it, always replied, "I will return to you in the stone." Korczak first had been told this story by another contemporary of Crazy Horse, Old Black Elk.

The story of the stone at the ear was one of the factors giving the mountain carving somewhat of a mystical aura from the outset of the project. Another was the fact Crazy Horse died September 6, 1877, and Korczak was born September 6, 1908. Some Indians read that as a sign Korczak was destined to return Crazy Horse in the stone. A pair of repeating cycles also came into play. While Korczak was born 31 years after Crazy Horse was killed, it was another 31 years until Standing Bear wrote Korczak inviting him to the Black Hills to carve Crazy Horse.

The year after the dedication, in September 1949, another colorful cere-

The first blast on Crazy Horse — at the peak of the mountain — was barely visible from the studio-home nearly a mile away. It took off a modest 10 tons of granite.

mony was held at Thunderhead Mountain. While representatives of the National Congress of American Indians, with their president Justice N. B. Johnson of Oklahoma, and government officials and tourists looked on, Ziolkowski blasted 20,000 tons of rock from the mountain with 1,000 pounds of dynamite. On this occasion, the National Congress of American Indians, which held its convention in Rapid City at the time, went on record as supporting the project with the full weight of its prestige and authority. The Black Hills Indian Council also endorsed Crazy Horse, as many other Indian organizations have done during the intervening years.

By this time, several national periodicals became interested in the memorial, and lent the light of their publicity to the enterprise. *TIME Magazine* carried a picture of the model of the memorial and a brief description titled "Big Chipper." *LIFE* devoted almost two pages to pictures of Korczak and the dedication ceremony. *The Minneapolis Sunday Tribune* ran a full-color page description of the opening ceremonies in its rotogravure section under the title "Sculptor Begins Crazy Horse Memorial."

It was the beginning of intense media interest in Crazy Horse and Korczak. Each year more and more print and broadcast journalists came from all over the world to report to the public on the unique humanitarian project unfolding at Crazy Horse. The resulting international publicity helped not only the non-profit project but had an incalculable impact on South Dakota's developing tourism industry.

While the Memorial had its supporters, it was not without local controversy. Korczak learned soon after his arrival in the Hills the Indian was not looked upon favorably by many whites in the area. He put it this way: "My biggest surprise out here was how they hated Indians with a purple passion. I had no idea. If I hadn't seen it with my own eyes, I wouldn't have believed it. I'm not an 'Indian lover.' I'm just a storyteller in stone, and the story of the

American Indian is a truly epic tale that needs telling. If you are going to live today for the future, you have to have an understanding of the past.

"I do think they got one helluva raw deal. This is one of the purposes of my work — I want to give them back a little more of their inherent pride, for with their pride intact they will be able to do for themselves and be the noble race they were. But, a lot of people hated me for wanting to tell the story. Those people tried everything they could think of to stop this project, made things very difficult for us — especially in the beginning. Still, they didn't treat me as badly as they treated Gutzon Borglum, whom I admired very much and whose work put them on the map. I know one thing; the racism was so strong out here, if it hadn't been for what Gutzon Borglum accomplished at Mt. Rushmore, I never could have moved one rock for an Indian Memorial in the Black Hills. The *Noah Webster Statue* helped prepare me for their attitude out here. I always say, 'None is so blind as he who will not see.' "

An Unprecedented Scale

Initially, Korczak planned to carve only the top 100 feet of the 600-foot-high mountain. But, after studying it, he felt a 100-foot-high carving on top of the big mountain would not look right; so, he decided to carve the entire monolith — *in the round*. Such a scale was unprecedented; no sculptor in the modern or ancient world ever conceived or undertook such a colossal carving.

The dimensions of the equestrian are astonishing. Overall it will be 563 feet high and 641 feet long. Crazy Horse's head will be nearly 90 feet high (indeed, all four of the 60-foot-high presidential heads on Mt. Rushmore would fit inside Crazy Horse's head). The Indian's outstretched arm will be 263 feet long (nearly the length of a football stadium) and 4,000 people could stand on the outstretched arm. When the opening between the horse's neck and the Indian's arm is completed, you could put a 10-story building inside it. The horse's head will be 219 feet high or as tall as a 22-story building, and a five room house would fit inside each of the horse's flaring nostrils. The pointing finger will be 37½ feet long and 10 feet thick, while the Indian's hand will be 33 feet thick. And, the poem Korczak wrote reflecting on "My lands are where my dead lie buried" will be carved on the mountain in letters three feet tall.

When Korczak planned to carve only the top 100 feet, he felt it might take about 10 years, depending on financing, the weather and other hard-to-predict factors. After deciding to make a carving nearly six times as large, he realized

The overleaf photographs taken spring, 1990 show the Crazy Horse mountain carving now in progress with approximately 8.3-million tons of granite blasted away blocking out the 563-foot-high sculpture in the round. Korczak's 1/34th scale model shows how the mountain will look when completed. The outline painted on the mountain also helps people visualize what will be carved. In 1989 eight lighting companies donated a lighting system, and the floodlights cast shadows which bring out the third dimensional aspect of Crazy Horse. By summer, 1990 the Indian's forehead was completed, smoothed by a 5,400-degree torch, and definition began on the Indian's eyes and nose. (Photos by Robb DeWall)

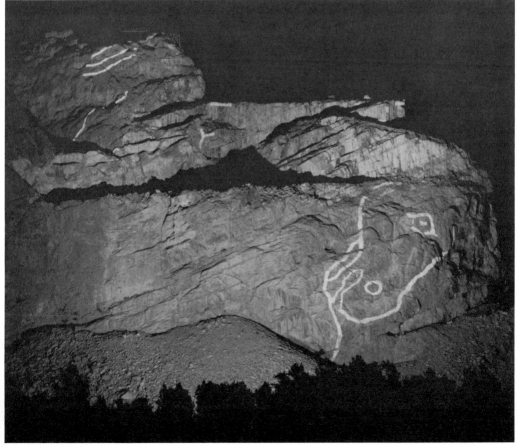

the project was much larger than any one man's lifetime. So, with his wife, Ruth, he drew up three books of measurements and detailed plans for the mountain carving with which he always said Crazy Horse could be completed.

A Free Enterprise Basis

Financing always has been the key to the progress at Crazy Horse. In the beginning Korczak felt the revenue to finance the work on the mountain could be raised from voluntary contributions from visitors to the Memorial. He got quite a shock when contributions the first year amounted to only five cents a person.

Although he did not want to charge any fee, directors of the non-profit Crazy Horse Foundation insisted an admission charge was necessary. Reluctantly, Korczak gave in and agreed to a small entrance charge of 50 cents a person. Over the years as costs and inflation rose steadily, directors often argued unsuccessfully for greater increases in the admission fee than Korczak would allow. He insisted the admission be kept as low as possible and still allow him to work on the mountain.

The Crazy Horse admission (since 1974 a per-CARload fee) consistently has been far below any other entrance fee in the area. Additionally, Korczak never would allow a charge for Indians, servicemen in uniform or residents of Custer County, in which the Memorial is located. From the beginning he also held an open house every spring and fall for South Dakota and Wyoming residents to visit Crazy Horse free of charge to view the annual progress. Crazy Horse always has been open on a year around basis, and visitors at Crazy Horse always have been offered free coffee because Korczak and Ruth felt the visitor must be treated as a guest in their home.

A strong believer in the free-enterprise system, Korczak always said, "This is a grassroots humanitarian project. If the interested public wants to come to Crazy Horse and pay that modest fee to finance the work, Crazy Horse will grow and progress."

He believed so strongly in free enterprise, he twice turned down 10 million dollars in potential Federal Government funding for Crazy Horse. He did not feel the taxpayer should have to finance his work. Additionally, he felt the Federal Government would neither finish the mountain carving nor carry out the project's humanitarian goals. He knew from first-hand experience the great difficulties Gutzon Borglum had working with Federal Government funding at Mt. Rushmore. And, he noted the work on Mt. Rushmore stopped when Borglum died (his last scale model for Mt. Rushmore shows he intended to carve the four full busts down to the waist).

Many of Korczak's friends urged him to take the federal money for Crazy Horse, but in spite of severe financial hardship he refused to even consider taking tax money, and steadfastly remained true to his free enterprise philosophy. During his lifetime he single-handedly raised and spent more than five million dollars on Crazy Horse, and proclaimed proudly that not a single penny of federal or state money was ever accepted or spent on the project. Additionally, during the more than three and one-half decades he worked on the mountain carving he never accepted a salary or personal expense account.

Making a Living

In the early days of the project the revenue was so limited Korczak had to turn to outside sources of income. He raised beef and pork for food and for sale. He acquired a few pure-bred registered Holsteins, and went into the dairy business. Korczak designed and built a modern milking-parlor, at the time one of the most up-to-date in a five-state area. From designing and blueprinting to digging and laying the foundation and cement blocks, all the work was done by the sculptor and Ruth. The same was true for a large lumber mill he constructed on the Crazy Horse property. He harvested, processed and sold lumber for a number of years. In addition to providing revenue, the mill served the dual purpose of supplying the large quantities of lumber he needed for the growing visitor complex and for the mountain. During the long winters he also accepted some sculptural commissions. Among them were two of the famous figures of the history of the American West.

His 1953 portrait of Sitting Bull figured in a "verbal war" between North and South Dakota that triggered headlines throughout the world. It started when the Medicine Man's three granddaughters decided their famous forefather should have his final resting place in South Dakota, where he had spent the major part of his life. Korczak agreed to make the memorial for the new grave.

Since his death in 1890, Sitting Bull's grave on the Indian reservation at Fort Yates, North Dakota, had been allowed to deteriorate badly. When the descendants applied for a disinterment permit to relocate the grave south of the border, North Dakota officials flatly refused — even though federal officials said the burial site was up to the descendants, who were meeting frequently with Korczak.

The group took matters into its own hands, and on a snowy pre-dawn April morning, armed with crowbars and shovels, they "stole" Sitting Bull's bones and whisked them to South Dakota where they were reburied on a majestic butte overlooking the Missouri River near Mobridge. Sitting Bull was perhaps the most famous American Indian in the world (owing largely to Buffalo Bill's Wild West Show in which he'd appeared for many years); so, when the story broke, it and the resulting controversy between North and South Dakota made front page national news for weeks. There wasn't much fear of Sitting Bull's bones being retaken, however, because they had been reburied under 20 tons of concrete on which was placed a six-ton pedestal to hold the seven-ton portrait Korczak had carved from one of the early Crazy Horse blast fragments.

Korczak quickly became a student of Black Hills history, and one of the more unusual portraits he carved at Crazy Horse was of the famous Deadwood marshal of gold-rush days, Wild Bill Hickok. It was carved in 1951 from a huge rock fragment blasted off the mountain. The sculptor made the portrait because Wild Bill was a part of the history of the Black Hills — and especially of Deadwood, some of whose residents had been helpful to Korczak after his arrival in the Hills.

The *Wild Bill Hickock* portrait is located across from the Adams Museum at the foot of Mt. Moriah where Wild Bill and Calamity Jane are buried. The statue also is on the site of Wild Bill's last camp. The sculptor carved in the stone on the back of the portrait, "Created as a gift by Korczak," but vandals have chipped off the "Created as a gift."

Another source of revenue for the mountain carving came from the sale of Crazy Horse souvenirs. Although he never wanted a gift shop, he reluctantly gave in to the visitor demands for postcards and souvenirs. He stipulated, however, that only Crazy Horse mementoes and Indian arts and crafts could be sold. Taking a chapter from the Noah Webster saga, he did permit the sale of small plaster models of Crazy Horse — which have been very popular over the years. Blast fragments from the mountain were offered without charge, but visitors taking them traditionally have made a small contribution for the work on the mountain.

A Family Project

Korczak came to the Black Hills with a single thought — to keep his promise to the old Indian Chiefs to carve a mountain to their great Chief Crazy Horse. The last thing he expected to happen was that he would get married and have a big family.

On Thanksgiving Day, 1950, he wed the former Ruth Ross from West Hartford, Connecticut. He was 42 and she was 24. She had been among the student volunteers on the Noah Webster Statue in 1941-42. She also had helped him mow lawns to finance the statue, and Ruth played drum in the Noah Webster Fife and Drum Corps, which she continued all during World War II while Korczak was in the service. She and several others from West Hartford had

The Ziolkowski family in 1969 — Korczak, Ruth, Marinka, Monique, Joel, Mark, Anne, Casimi

36

helped the sculptor move west in 1947, and she stayed to help in any way possible at Crazy Horse. She started by peeling all the logs he felled to build the original log cabin studio-home. Before they married, he told her he had to keep his promises to the old Indians, so the mountain always would come first. She replied that was all right with her, and it always was.

As the years passed, they had 10 children — five boys and five girls, all born at Crazy Horse. Korczak delivered one of them himself. As they grew, there were so many Ziolkowskis in school at one time, Korczak bought an old one-room country schoolhouse, and moved it to Crazy Horse. Six of their youngsters went to the Crazy Horse school, where they were taught by a certified teacher.

Carving Thunderhead Mountain

The dedication blast in 1948 was the only blast on the mountain that year because several major obstacles remained to be overcome before Korczak could begin the job for which he came to the Black Hills — carving a mountain.

Having spent all of his first year building a place to live and to accommodate visitors, sinking a well and bringing in a "road" from the distant highway, he had to turn his attentions the second year to the problems of providing access to and up the 600-foot-high mountain, of getting some equipment to begin work on it — and of doing all this with virtually no money.

Solving the latter problem was relatively easy — he again did all the work

Jadwiga, Adam, Dawn and John.

himself. It was a long, backbreaking ordeal, but those first two solitary years at Crazy Horse set the stage and began to prepare Korczak for the many obstacles he would face during the more than three decades he would labor on the mountain.

Korczak had to build the studio-home about a mile from the mountain to keep it at a safe distance from the blasting. Clearing the first road over to the mountain took a great deal of time and effort because he had to cut through a mile of dense timber. When he got to the bottom of the mountain, there still was the problem of how to get up and down the 600-foot-high monolith.

Initially, he rode horseback part way up the far side of the mountain, then climbed to the top on a rope — carrying his tools on his back. This was how he had prepared the first blast, for which he "single-jacked" the drill holes by hand with a hammer and chisel.

His answer to the problem of getting up the mountain was a singular one: he designed and built a 700-foot-long staircase which ran from the valley floor all the way to the top of the mountain. Using the timber cleared from the road to the mountain, Korczak carried up, on his back, an estimated 29 tons of green lumber for the staircase.

The work was done during the bitter cold winter in 1948-49, which included the great Blizzard of '49, and Ruth assisted him on the project. When it was finished, the staircase had 741 steps. The last one was at an elevation of 6,740 feet above sea level at the top of the mountain.

He used the long staircase for many years, carrying his tools on his back up and down the 741 steps. Although building it was an extraordinary challenge, it was Korczak's typically pragmatic solution to a difficult problem, compounded by lack of revenue and the worst possible weather conditions. And, the story of the staircase — built virtually for the price of a few nails — is a prime example of how Korczak employed his imagination, ingenuity, engineering skill and great physical and mental strength to overcome so many of the obstacles he would face in the decades he worked on the mountain carving.

Korczak's first two pieces of equipment for the mountain were a small, used jackhammer and an old gasoline powered Buda compressor that stood at the bottom of the mountain. To get the compressed air up the mountain to power his jackhammer he had to lay a pipeline 2040 feet long around the base, up the far side and over the top of the mountain.

Finally, after two years of exhausting groundwork, Korczak was able to begin carving the mountain the summer of 1949. During the short season he blasted 97,000 tons of rock off the mountain. He started at the top of the Indian's head, having made an "educated" guess at the location of the Indian's nose. Korczak always had a keen sense of proportion, so it was no surprise the guess was accurate. All future measurements on the huge mountain carving were made in reference to the Indian's nose.

He was no stranger to the skills required for mountain carving. Korczak always said his whole life had prepared him for the Crazy Horse project. In his early life helping his foster father in the construction business and, later, working many years on the Boston docks, he learned or observed a wide variety of engineering and construction skills including the use of heavy equipment and explosives. He called on many of those skills in designing, erecting and creating the 22-ton *Noah Webster Statue,* and he used and refined many of them during the war — especially the use of dynamite. It was that background of knowledge and experience he put to work when he began Crazy Horse.

That year, 1949, Crazy Horse visitation totalled 102,000 people. Many had difficulty visualizing where Crazy Horse was going to be carved on the huge mountain. At that time they had only Korczak's small 1/300 size scale model for a point of reference. So, to help people understand what he was carving, Korczak decided to paint an outline of the massive "equestrian" on the huge mountainside.

Swinging down hand over hand on a one-inch rope with a bucket of paint tied to his belt, a brush in one hand, and an army field telephone strapped to his back, he spent much of the summer of 1950 completing the outline. Because he was right on the mountain, he could not keep his perspective on the big outline, so Ruth, at the studio-home nearly a mile away, used the surveying instruments and communicated directions to him over the field telephone. To make the outline clearly visible from the studio-home, he had to paint the lines an average of six feet wide; over 174 gallons of paint were used. Blasting and the weather eroded the outline away in just a few years.

Working alone dawn to dusk during the brief summers, Korczak spent the next five seasons blasting out the rough profile of the Indian's nearly 90-foot-high head. This removed 630-thousand tons of rock from the mountain.

Realizing he would need a bulldozer on top of the mountain to help clear the rock from above the Indian's outstretched arm, he spent the entire winter of 1956-57 blasting out a road up the back of the mountain. His wife's birthday present that year (on June 26th) was the first ride to the top of the mountain in the bulldozer, which thrilled her even though she was seven months pregnant. The new road enabled him to drive to work at the top in a jeep instead of using the long staircase to carry up all his tools and equipment on his back — as he did for the first six years. He also was able to move the old Buda to the top where the shorter air line provided greater power.

Bulldozing on top of the 600-foot-high mountain provided new perils. But, he had no choice because the dynamite blasts left huge blast fragments on the 42-foot-wide arm. So, the cycle of drilling, blasting and bulldozing began. And, when he finished clearing the arm — in 1963 — approximately two million tons of rock had been removed.

The unusual sight of a bulldozer atop the mountain provided exciting viewing for visitors. Korczak would hang a big blade out in space as he nudged over the edge heavy boulders that cascaded loudly down into the valley far below. The sight also pointed up one of the several major differences between Crazy Horse and nearby Mt. Rushmore. No bulldozers ever were required on Rushmore because all the blast fragments fell away from the work areas. A few of the many other interesting differences between the two mountain carvings are:

Rushmore is grey pegmatite granite, mostly high bas-relief, 60 feet high (about 450,000 tons of rock were removed), and federally financed; Crazy Horse is reddish pegmatite granite, sculpture in the round, 563 feet high (an estimated eight and one-half million tons of rock will be removed), and financed through the free enterprise system as part of a non-profit humanitarian project. Additionally, the Shrine of Democracy tells one part of American history while Crazy Hose tells another part. Both sculptors were American-born sons of immigrants — Borglum of Danish parents, Korczak of Polish parents.

The road to the top of Crazy Horse, the heavier equipment and having electricity on the mountain were tremendous helps in speeding up the progress on the mountain. As his family grew, the children also began to help. His young sons worked with him on the mountain while the girls helped their mother at the visitor center. The dairy farm continued for many years, and the youngsters also were a great help tending and milking the cattle, which provided all the milk and meat for the growing family as well as revenue for the project.

Ruth was spending most of her days explaining to visitors what Korczak was carving on the mountain. She had only his small marble 1/300 scale model of Crazy Horse for a point of reference, so her task was made considerably easier in the mid 1960's when Korczak made the large plaster 1/34 scale model for the mountain carving (shown on the front cover of this booklet). It weighs 16 tons, and he built it on a platform mounted on railroad wheels and tracks so it could be outside in clear weather and rolled back under cover in wet weather.

With the Indian's profile roughed out and the arm cleared, Korczak's next work on the mountain was blasting an opening under the Indian's arm and carving out the top of the horse's mane. Digging the 110-foot-long tunnel through the mountain was what Korczak called "hard rock mining at its worst." Just to get to daylight took him two suffocating years and required the removal of about 400,000 tons of rock. After blasts, much of it had to be carried out of the tunnel by wheelbarrow. A further frustration to him was that during the two years he was laboring in the tunnel out of public view, some people said he had stopped working on the mountain.

Expanding the tunnel and *roughing out* the 62-foot-high horse's mane — which involved some very dangerous bulldozing 500 feet up the mountain — took another 800,000 tons off the mountain — and consumed the rest of the decade of the 1960's. After more than 20 solitary years of slow but steady progress on the mountain during the short summers, Korczak reached a pair of milestones in 1971: he began work on the 219-foot-high horse's head and the Crazy Horse project was out of debt for the first time. Korczak was 63, and it also was the year he made a gesture toward the inevitable — starting work on his tomb.

By 1971 Korczak had blasted approximately 3,200,000 tons of rock off the mountain *roughing out* the 563-foot-high equestrian in the round. Using mining engineering technics his first goal was to block out the entire figure of Crazy Horse to within 10-12 feet of the finish surface, leaving that much "cushion" of rock to protect the more than two miles of surface from the heaviest blasting.

He started at the top and worked downward — first blocking out the Indian's 90-foot-high head, next clearing the 263-foot-long outstretched arm, and then tunnelling through the solid granite mountain to start the huge opening under the arm. The next step — the 22-story-high horse's head — was a challenge Korczak had awaited eagerly. No one ever before had attempted to carve the head of a horse on such a gigantic scale. Korczak undertook the mammoth task with gusto. What was required was removal of virtually the entire east quarter of the huge mountain and removal of another 4,000,000 tons of rock — just for the horse's head. To accomplish that, the sculptor and his sons carried out a long decade of the heaviest blasting and bulldozing on the project. On September 6, 1977, the Centennial of Crazy Horse's death, the largest single blast of the project blew 40,000 tons of rock off the mountain. Some of the drill holes were 70 feet deep. The spectacular explosion threw boulders nearly three-fourths of a mile, narrowly missing the sculptor (observing his 69th birthday) and slightly injuring one member of a television crew photographing the blast.

To "dig out" the horse's head, Korczak required additional heavy equipment. By making many sacrifices, he was able in the late 1960's to buy a new twin electric compressor to power his drilling equipment. It was installed near the top of the mountain, and provided greatly increased compression power — which was a major factor in speeding up the progress on the mountain. Because of the financial limitations with which he constantly struggled, most of Korczak's equipment was bought second hand. He restored or rebuilt the machinery in his garage during the long winters.

The rolling stock grew and grew, eventually including several large and small Caterpillar bulldozers, a loader, two wagon drills and an air-trac. A little-understood aspect of mountain carving is the number of pieces of heavy equipment required. Today the Crazy Horse equipment fleet totals about 80 vehicles, machines, and compressors ranging from small jeeps to a 45-ton crane with a 125-foot boom and a 72-ton Caterpillar.

Another little-appreciated aspect of Korczak's work at Crazy Horse was the extensive roadbuilding he had to do. Overall, he built more than five and one-half miles of roads just to get to and up the mountain carving. Heavy rains frequently eroded away his roads, forcing him to rebuild them several times a year. On just the horse's head, he had to build five separate roads to get to work areas, which continuously were blasted away as he progressed down the 219-foot head.

Roadwork was a constant frustration to Korczak, who estimated he spent almost half his time at Crazy Horse building and maintaining the extensive road network he had to have on and off the mountain. That included the Charles Anthony Morss Bridge to Crazy Horse. It took Korczak 17 years to get permission to build it above the railroad tracks near the Crazy Horse entrance. The big concrete bridge is named for Korczak's great friend and benefactor.

While the mountain was changing dramatically, so was Korczak. He suffered numerous injuries working on the mountain carving, and there were more close calls than he cared to recall. Still, he always said he never would be killed on the mountain because he had the feeling Crazy Horse was watching over him. He wasn't alone; many Indians who visited the mountain told him they felt Crazy Horse's presence.

Already 40 years old when he began work on the mountain, he brought with him several injuries suffered during the many years he played football, baseball and hockey during his younger life. Additionally, he was seriously wounded twice during the war, and each wound left its mark.

The years of jackhammering and bulldozing on Thunderhead Mountain

One of the Ziolkowski children's favorite pictures of their father, pausing atop the mountain carving after a long day's work. He quipped, "They would like one where I'm sitting down on the job!"

also took their toll. He underwent four separate back operations between 1962 and 1980 (when he was 72) for the removal of six consecutive discs in his lower back. But, he ignored the pain and continued working.

He also suffered two heart attacks — a slight one in 1968 and a massive one in 1970 (when he was 62). Each time he returned to work, although arthritis and diabetes were additional complications that made daily life painful. He also suffered a score of "smaller injuries" such as broken fingers, a broken wrist, broken arms, legs, ribs, and he suffered impaired hearing due to the 40mm guns while he was in the Army and the years of drilling and blasting on the mountain. He also tore ligaments and, in an ill-advised step off a bulldozer, ruptured his Achilles' tendon. That forced him to wear a heavy cast on his leg and foot one summer. Nevertheless, he bulldozed as usual on the mountain all season, in spite of the cast. He had done it before with other breaks and other casts.

In addition to ignoring his many injuries, Korczak also defied advancing age to continue working with his sons on Crazy Horse, which the 1976 *Reader's Digest U.S. Bicentennial Book* listed as "one of the seven wonders of the modern world." In 1978 he worked as usual on the horse's head as the 30th anniversay of the dedication of the mountain carving and his 70th birthday came and went. Of the approximately four and one-half billion people on the planet Earth, Korczak was the only one carving a mountain.

By the end of the 1970's he had blasted about 7,000,000 tons of rock off the mountain, and much of the rough form of the 22-story-high horse's head was emerging against the sky. And, as the 1980's arrived, Korczak was cutting in under the vast and dangerous overhang of the mountain to begin lifting out the horse's nose and left eye. Meanwhile, with his great progress dramatically apparent on the mountain carving, and with the ever-expanding visitor complex offering "something for everyone," 1981 visitation topped one million for the first time.

What the visitor finds at Crazy Horse is virtually a small town built up by Korczak over the years. The focal point of the sprawling visitor complex is his large scale model for the mountain carving, which can be viewed from a large covered viewing veranda. Apart from viewing the work on the mountain, there is much for visitors to see in the rambling complex. It has grown to more than 61 rooms, many filled with Korczak's wood and marble works of sculpture and his extensive collection of beautiful antiques. Among his works is the 55-piece grandfather's clock Korczak made at age 18, and which so captivated Judge Cabot.

From the original log studio-home he built while living in a tent the year he arrived at Crazy Horse, the visitor complex has grown to include his large workshop, the Indian Museum of North America, the Indian Arts and Crafts Gallery, a small Crazy Horse gift shop, a snack bar (offering the traditional free coffee to everyone), twin theaters and large, beautiful restrooms. Crazy Horse even features an Egyptian Room, housing exact replicas of major pieces of furniture found in King Tut's tomb. The unique collection was given to Korczak and Ruth. The complex also houses the private living quarters of the Ziolkowski family.

Lining the walkway to the studio-home (still open to the public) is an outdoor sculpture gallery with many of the marble portraits he carved in the East — a reminder of the studio career he gave up to devote the rest of his life to the Crazy Horse project. In 1982 Korczak created, designed and built the elaborate Black Hills Nature Gates near his studio-home. They measure 24 feet high and nearly 50 feet long. Under his direction a son and daughter of the sculptor drew, hand-cut and etched to insert into the gates more than 210 brass silhouettes of birds, animals, fish, plants, flowers and trees native to the Black Hills area.

In 1982 he conducted experiments with a 5,400-degree Fahrenheit torch to be used in carving the horse's left eye. Korczak designed and built a 20-foot-high steel templet to help him carve the perfect curve of the horse's left eye, which bulges out from the mountain about 18 feet, is taller than a two-story building and about 30 feet wide. Ultimately, all of the more than two miles of finish surface on Crazy Horse will be heated with the torch to seal and glaze the granite.

The summer of '82 Korczak underwent a successful quadruple heart by-pass operation, and observed his 74th birthday Sept. 6th supervising the painting on the mountain of a new outline of the horse's head, to be used as a point of reference for drilling on the head. Several of his children did the painting by rappelling down the mountain or working from "spiders," small electric work platforms running up and down the mountain on cable. The spiders were among several pieces of long-needed heavy equipment Korczak acquired after his return from heart surgery. They included a used 45-ton crane with a 125-foot boom to be used to elevate a large work platform up and down the 22-story height of the emerging horse's head — beside which the giant machine looked like an erector set toy. An unlikely sculptural tool, it was the latest example of Korczak's innovativeness in combining engineering and sculpting.

The full impact of Korczak's great progress on the mountain carving was brought home with the cut under the horse's nose and with the new outline on the mountain pinpointing the position of the 219-foot-high horse's head on which he'd spent more than a decade. After nearly 36 years of backbreaking — and sometimes heartbreaking — labor, Korczak had blasted off a total of approximately 7,200,00 tons of rock *blocking out* the 563-foot-high figure in the round, and the colossal equestrian was beginning to emerge in rough form against the sky. He calculated that during those 36 years he actually had been able to work on the mountain only 16-17 full years, if all the time lost to the long winters and pioneering were subtracted.

In spite of the many obstacles he faced — severe financial hardships, injuries, illnesses, advancing age, racism and fickle Mother Nature — Korczak had no regrets. He said, "I would do it all over again. The treatment of the American Indian is the blackest mark on the escutcheon of our nation's history. By carving Crazy Horse, if I can give back to the Indian some of his pride and create the means to keep alive his culture and heritage, my life will have been worthwhile."

A practical man, Korczak carefully prepared the Crazy Horse project and his large family for his death. When it came unexpectedly October 20, 1982, he was laid to rest in a tomb near the base of the mountain. Working on and off during the winter months, Korczak and his sons had blasted it out of a large outcropping on which the permanent Indian Museum of North America will be located one day. When the tomb neared completion in 1980, it was consecrated by the Catholic Church. Korczak's wife didn't care much for the idea of the tomb when he started it, but she conceded it was "like carrying an umbrella so it won't rain." The sculptor also built his own pine casket, and it was on public display in his workshop for several years.

In explaining the tomb, Korczak said, "I always want to be near the mountain so I can see the progress and watch the humanitarian phases of Crazy Horse grow and grow. It will take much hard work and many years to complete, maybe many lifetimes, but Crazy Horse can and will be completed because it is right that it should be done."

Typically, Korczak made all the arrangements in advance for his own funeral, which was held outside on the viewing veranda in front of his large scale model for Crazy Horse and in full view of the mountain carving. It was a beautiful Indian summer day, and circling the mountain during the ceremony were three eagles, good luck omens to the Indians. And, a solitary, lone eagle floated overhead as Korczak's body was driven to the mountain the last time. His wife, Ruth — the "little girl" he met on the Noah Webster Statue — and all 10 of their children were with him as he was laid to rest.

A man of great humor, Korczak wanted the last laugh, so he had a brass door knocker placed on the *inside* of the tomb door. And, he wrote his own epitaph, and hand cut it from three-quarter-inch-thick steel. It reads:

The Purpose of Crazy Horse

As the mountain progressed, Korczak also worked hard to advance the cultural and educational phases of his Crazy Horse humanitarian dream.

The winter of 1972-73 he and his sons built the first phase of the Indian Museum of North America. The beautiful structure — 100 feet long, 65 feet wide, and with a 25-foot-high ceiling — was built entirely from native pine Korczak harvested from around the mountain. It houses more than 1,000 artifacts representing more than 50 Indian tribes. Most of the collection has been donated. (Donations to Crazy Horse — artifacts, books, equipment, monetary and other — are deductible from the donor's federal income tax because Crazy Horse Memorial is a non-profit, educational, humanitarian Foundation.)

In keeping with Korczak's master plan for the project, the permanent Indian museum will be built near the mountain when the heavy blasting is completed. Architecturally unusual, it will be a vast hogan — a multi-storied circular building 350 feet in diameter with the traditional circular opening in the rounded roof. It will be built from Crazy Horse blast fragments, and will house a definitive collection of artifacts telling the remarkable story of the culture of the American Indian.

In 1979 he also launched the educational part of the project by establishing the Crazy Horse Memorial Indian Scholarship program. In announcing the program, which since has provided scores of scholarships to Indian students, Korczak said, "Some may say I should not divert this money from the mountain carving, but after more than three decades of work and progress on the mountain, I think I should be allowed this small pittance toward the long range educational goals. I do it as a good faith gesture to the old Indians who invited me to the Black Hills. I promised them this would be a humanitarian project, and I have dedicated my life to keeping my promise."

The sculptor stipulated the funding for the scholarships be kept in line percentage-wise with the gross amount of gate receipts, together with the sale of Crazy Horse souvenirs and Indian arts and crafts. The scholarships are administered by the participating colleges, universities, vo-tec and nursing schools, which also select the recipients.

Eventually, the University and Medical Training Center for the North American Indian will rise near the mountain. It will be an imposing complex separated by the Avenue of the Chiefs leading visitors to the Indian Museum on the shore of the large reflecting pool around the base of the mountain carving. The Avenue will be lined with stone portraits of famous Indian Chiefs from many of the Indian tribes throughout the nation — not just the Sioux. The University and Medical Training Center will be perpetually endowed by the ongoing admission fee after the mountain carving is completed. In specifying medical training as one of the educational specialties to be offered, Korczak was recognizing one of the Indian's greatest natural gifts—healing.

A Gift to the Future

Sculptor Korczak Ziolkowski was a visionary man who planned beyond his lifetime. Thus, when he died, his Crazy Horse dream did not die with him. It's a measure of the man. He devoted his life to a project he knew he could not live to see completed, yet he believed so strongly in the justness of the Crazy Horse dream, he was able to trust its fulfillment to the future—to his wife, his large family, and friends and strangers who, now and in the future, share his humanitarian vision.

At the outset, when he realized the project was larger than any one man's lifetime, he set down detailed plans and instructions for the future. With Ruth, he drew up three books of measurements and "blueprint type" specifications for the mountain carving with which he always said Crazy Horse could be completed. Together, they also formulated the master plan for the project.

As he planned, the work today is being carried out under the capable direction of Ruth, and their large family in conjunction with the Crazy Horse Memorial Foundation Directors. It's a task to which Ruth brought a lifetime of experience after more than three decades not only as wife and mother but as Korczak's closest friend and associate in every aspect of Crazy Horse Memorial — from its humble beginning.

While shunning the spotlight for herself, she was at Korczak's side every step of the way at Crazy Horse, helping pioneer and build (staircase, roads, dairy, lumber mill, visitor complex), prepare the three measurement books with which to complete the mountain, formulate the Crazy Horse master plan, run the business affairs (as Secretay-Treasurer of the Crazy Horse Memorial Foundation), purchase the light and heavy equipment and order all the repair parts, manage the visitor complex, and serve as "hostess to the world" meeting the general public, the news media and the VIP's.

Both knew, because Ruth was 18 years younger, the great responsibility for carrying on Korczak's life's work one day might pass to her and their large family. They planned accordingly. He was an extraordinary teacher. She was an exceptional student. He expressed great confidence in her natural and acquired

Korczak and Ruth Ziolkowski. She first met him in West Hartford, Conn., when she was 13 years old.

abilities; indeed, Korczak's last words to Ruth were, "You must work on the mountain, but you must do it slowly — so you do it right."

Ruth says, "Korczak's life would be wasted if Crazy Horse is not completed. He gave the project not only its inspiration but, after more than 35 years of hard work, enormous momentum for the future. He left us all the plans and a wealth of ideas for the future; relying on those and his free enterprise philosophy, we are dedicated to carrying on his work.

"From the beginning he always said, 'this is a grassroots project; if the interested public continues to come here and pay that modest admission fee to finance the work, Crazy Horse can be finished.' He told us exactly what to do and how to go about it, so we feel '*he still walks here.*' Korczak's dream is very much alive and his work is progressing every day."

Quotations from Korczak

Only in America could a man carve a mountain.

⌐~つ

The treatment of the American Indian is the blackest mark on the escutcheon of our nation's history. By carving Crazy Horse, if I can give back to the Indian some of his pride and create the means to keep alive his culture and heritage, my life will have been worthwhile.

⌐~つ

It's all very well to be well descended, but the glory belongs to our ancestors.

⌐~つ

Every man has his mountain — I'm carving mine.

⌐~つ

The world asks you one question: did you do your job? The answer is not: I would have done it if people had been nicer . . . if I'd had the money . . . if I hadn't died; if's don't count. The answer must be: yes!

⌐~つ

To you I give this granite epic
for your descendants always to know
'My lands are where my dead lie buried.'

⌐~つ

When the legends die, the dreams end;
        when the dreams end, there is no more greatness.

Appendix

any honors were bestowed on Korczak during his lifetime, including membership in the National Sculpture Society, but during the long years he toiled on Crazy Horse, he drew his greatest encouragement from the grassroots support of his work. Much of it was expressed in letters that arrived each day from people throughout the world, many enclosing a few dollars or more to further his work. He said their faith in what he was doing was a source of strength to him. He especially enjoyed hearing from youngsters, scores of whom wrote each year, often enclosing proceeds from special projects they conducted to raise funds to further Crazy Horse.*

Among his many honors were an Honorary Doctorate of Fine Arts from Fairfield University, Connecticut (1970), an Honorary Doctorate of Humane Letters from Black Hills State College, Spearfish, S.D. (1981) and the Trustee Award from the National Western Heritage and Cowboy Hall of Fame, Oklahoma City, Oklahoma (1974). But, perhaps the honor which gave him the greatest satisfaction was one for Crazy Horse.

On January 15, 1982, the U. S. Postal Service released the 13-cent Crazy Horse postage stamp. The first day of issue ceremony for the regular issue (post card denomination) stamp was held in the Indian Museum of North America at Crazy Horse. The portrait on the stamp was sketched from Korczak's large scale model for the mountain carving, and the stamp design was unveiled at Crazy Horse on Korczak's 73rd birthday, Sept. 6, 1981. The following are

---

*The hardbacked book *CRAZY HORSE AND KORCZAK: The Story of an Epic Mountain Carving* by Robb DeWall with Illustrations by Marinka Ziolkowski (160 pp. including 30 pp. of photographs of Korczak's sculpture and the mountain carving) answers the 12 most-asked questions by young people about the mountain carving and Korczak. The book, which critics and adult readers praise as being of interest to all age groups, is available only at Crazy Horse. Its publication was Ruth's gift to Korczak on the 35th anniversay of his May 3, 1947, arrival in the Black Hills to begin Crazy Horse. In it Korczak takes a visiting youngster on a thrilling tour of the mountain carving — including a ride in his bulldozer — during which the sculptor vividly relates how and why he undertook Crazy Horse.

remarks by Assistant U. S. Postmaster General Eugene C. Hagburg, the main speaker at the unveiling and first day of issue ceremonies:

Crazy Horse Stamp

Thank you and good morning, distinguished guests, ladies and gentlemen. I am delighted to be able to share this occasion with you and to have the privilege of representing Postmaster General William F. Bolger and the Postal Service at the first day of issue ceremony for the Crazy Horse Stamp. And, it is a distinct pleasure to be in the company of two unique and beautiful people — Korczak and Ruth Ziolkowski.

Actions speak louder than the most eloquent words. And what we say here this morning is not nearly as important as what we are doing. This is because the stamp we are dedicating honors a noble person — a noble people — and it will travel around the world communicating to one and all that the United States Postal Service recognizes Crazy Horse not only as a great American Indian leader, but also as a Great American.

Much of what I am going to say today, I said at the design unveiling. But I firmly believe that good words, like good deeds, bear repeating. Tradition, in fact, tells us that many stories told and retold become as important to our legacies from the past as do those words that are written. That words have been written does not necessarily make them true; some written histories have been known to be narrow, distorted, biased.

Because we recognize the great power stamps have to convey messages to millions of people in a graphic and immediate way, we feel a keen sense of responsibility when it comes to selecting the subjects they portray.

And while most men and women honored in this way have names and faces that are familiar to the majority of Americans, the Postal Service also uses stamps as tools to help bring wider recognition to those individuals and groups who have made significant contributions to our country but whose character and accomplishments are not as well known as they should be.

We believe that America's history should not be the history of only *some* Americans. We also believe that a knowledge, an understanding of the past, will help us to enhance the present and plan wisely for the future.

While the physical size of a postage stamp is small, its impact is great. Because stamps are seen and used and even saved by so many people, they have a very special power to communicate messages in an immediate and graphic way. And, we know that frequently stamps stimulate people to learn more about the subjects they portray. And we are optimistic this stamp will bring the proud name of the revered Oglala leader, Crazy Horse, the wide national and international attention and recognition that he has long deserved, and that because of this stamp human beings throughout the world — and especially young Americans — will come to learn more about Crazy Horse, the people from whom he came and for whom he both lived and died.

Our nation has many ways of honoring distinguished Americans and marking historic and meaningful events. One of the highest, most visible and longest lasting tributes is the very special honor roll of men and women who have been portrayed on United States postage stamps.

With the issuance of the Crazy Horse stamp in the great American series, one of history's most able military tacticians is welcomed into that select group of outstanding individuals that make up that special honor roll. A stamp is especially appropriate for Crazy Horse because a stamp is in a very real sense a living tribute. Stamps are part of our everyday lives . . . and even after they are no longer used, they are also a visual part of our nation's archives.

It is time my fellow Americans learn more about Crazy Horse and the Oglala people — their traditions, their ideals, their philosophy of life. All of these involve themes that are without question relevant to us today.

Korczak and Assistant U. S. Postmaster General Eugene C. Hagburg at the First Day of Issue Ceremony for the Crazy Horse stamp, sketched from the sculptor's large scale model for the mountain carving.

Inventions may have changed our world significantly in the last century . . . forms of transportation and communication . . . the ways we produce and prepare our food, clothing and shelter . . . these have gone beyond the imagination of our forefathers, in some cases even our parents never experienced or envisioned what we have become casually accustomed to.

But while many of the *things* in our lives have changed, the feelings we share as human beings . . . the life cycle . . . the passages, beginnings and endings, disappointments and dreams, these have not changed, despite all the years and the many things that are different.

Our stamp program is evidence of our belief that the present is sometimes best understood and enhanced by a clear vision of the past. Understanding the people and events of the past helps us to realize that we are all much more alike than we are differnt . . . and that the greatest dreams of our greatest heroes are those that do not advocate the building of walls to separate us from one another, but rather those that encourage the development of warmth and friendship that serve to unite us in spirit and sympathy.

And it is our hope that this stamp, this stamp depicting the noble face of Crazy Horse, will inspire more human beings to recognize all that we share as human beings. To learn more about Crazy Horse and his heritage will enrich our lives and add to the cultural wealth of our country.

In this regard, I want to mention the names of three books that focus on Crazy Horse. The first book, *Crazy Horse, Strange Man of the Oglala,* was written by the late Mari Sandoz, and the second and more recent one is titled, *Great Upon the Mountain.* It was written by Vinson Brown.

Both these works tell us about Crazy Horse as boy and man, as a spiritual as well as a military leader. They explain why he ranks so high in the esteem of his people and so well merits the honor we are according him with this stamp.

The third book is entitled *Land of the Spotted Eagle* by Luther Standing Bear. In it, the author tells how he was brought up. He discusses the values he was taught to respect and live by . . . the very same values by which Crazy Horse was raised and to which he held himself accountable.

It is a book I wish every youngster in our country would come across, particularly those who have never had an opportunity to learn of the beauty and the richness of the way of life led by Crazy Horse's people. The book teaches that although civilizations may differ outwardly in many ways, this does not mean that one is any the less civilized

I was particularly impressed with the passage in the book regarding the qualities of a brave, and I would like to share the gist of that passage with you, keeping in mind that Crazy Horse was considered the epitome of those characteristics.

To become a great brave was the highest aspiration and called for the greatest efforts. A brave not only had to be physically brave and an able fighter, he had to meet the severest tests of character. The great brave was and I quote: "a man of strict honor, undoubted truthfulness and unbound generosity." He had to be strong enough to part with his last horse or weapon and last bit of food. While he carried himeself with pride and dignity, he was without arrogance. He could endure pain, bear the scars of life, defy the elements, and laugh and sing in the face of death. He was a man of great courage.

There were no social strata among Crazy Horse's people that were unattainable by reason of class or birth, but those who demonstrated high intelligence and worthy character were recognized. And those who were better able to get along in the world did not wait to be asked for help, but rather took pride in providing it before requests for aid were necessary. Achievement was its own reward, and humaneness was not a law to be obeyed; it was an ideal to be lived.

The boy "Curly" became known as the man Crazy Horse because he was gifted with a special kind of insight and a vibrant spark that sustained his intense sense of responsibility not only to his immediate family but to all of his people . . . and to the vision he had in which he saw that ultimately all mankind would be united in good will.

Yes, we are honoring Crazy Horse because he was one of history's most able military tacticians. At the same time, I think it is important to recall *why* he fought as well as *how*.

Crazy Horse was a hero not only because of his military skill, but because of his strength of character and depth of vision. His people speak not only of how he trained his men and led them in battle, but of how he never abandoned his wounded and how he treated the elderly, the ill, the widowed and the children. He fought valiantly for two reasons: to protect the very lives of his people, and to preserve their valued way of life.

To understand the history of Crazy Horse is to better comprehend humanness. It is to witness pain and to respect the power of the human spirit to endure and triumph.

Though the years of Crazy Horse's life fell short of four decades, his courage, conviction and sense of commitment have lived on to inspire others. As long as human beings value loyalty and life, they will share Crazy Horse's glorious vision of a world of freedom, peace and human dignity for all children of the Great Spirit.

As I have said, that the Postal Service is honoring Crazy Horse in the stamp series entitled Great Americans, signals to all Americans that American history should indeed reflect the creativity, courage and culture of *all* Americans.

Mr. Korczak Ziolkowski's magnificent endeavor, carving a sculpture from Thunderhead Mountain to honor Crazy Horse, his people and their heritage, is more than just commendable. It is in itself monumental, herculean. In one sense it is beyond comprehension and yet so real. His vision and enthusiasm is contagious and we respect him for his extraordinary talent, skill, persistence and dedication. His will be *the* tribute for all time for Crazy Horse, a man who was a giant in spirit and strength, and who was indeed of and for this land he loved so well.

And Korczak Ziolkowski's vision of what will be will enrich our lives and culture forever.

The Great Americans series was launched in December 1980. Crazy Horse is the second North American Indian to be honored in it. Other stamps in the series have honored George Mason, who drafted the U. S. Bill of Rights, Rachel Carson, author and environmentalist, Dr. Charles R. Drew, black physician and medical researcher, and Dr. Ralph J. Bunche, black international diplomat and humanitarian. Sequoyah, the Cherokee Indian scholar who invented an alphabet for his tribe, launched the series in 1980. I might add that I had the privilege of dedicating that stamp, too.

The stamps in this series are what we call regular stamps. They differ from commemorative stamps which are on sale usually for about 90 days. Regular stamps, printed in larger quantities generally remain on sale at post office windows for much longer periods of time. (Years rather than months, so about one *billion* Crazy Horse stamps will be released during the lifetime of the issue.)

I would also like to point out that the Crazy Horse stamp bears the 13-cent postal card rate. This means that it is likely many people will use it to share news of their travels with family and friends, and undoubtedly many of these post cards will be mailed from right here at the U.S. Post Office at Crazy Horse, South Dakota.

And it is also fitting that we come to Crazy Horse, South Dakota, to issue this stamp. Because the Crazy Horse stamp can be acquired nowhere else in the world today. Beginning tomorrow, we will have a special crew responding to the thousands of request for the special cancellation that identifies this city and this day. And, since all future philatelic annals will record that on January 15, 1982, at Crazy Horse, South Dakota, a stamp in the Great Americans series was issued to honor the Great American called Crazy Horse, I like to think that he would be more than a little pleased.

And, now a word about stamp design. Few people realize how difficult it is to capture in the small space of a postage stamp the essence of a personality. But, I think that is exactly what Mr. Brad Holland has done. His sketch was drawn from Mr. Ziolkowski's large scale model for the Crazy Horse mountain carving. Although there are no photographs of Crazy Horse, Mr. Ziolkowski's portrait of him was based on detailed descriptions of Crazy Horse given the sculptor by contemporaries of the Sioux Chief.

This portrayal enables us to see the courage and determination of that rare human being — it is a countenance to be long remembered.

Now it is my pleasure to present albums containing the Crazy Horse stamp to the following distinguished persons:

The first, by tradition, goes to the President of the United States, and Mr. Reagan's will be delivered to the White House. The second I'm pleased to present to Mr. Ziolkowski, the third to the Indian Museum of North America here at Crazy Horse and the fourth to the U.S. Post Office at Crazy Horse for which Ruth Ziolkowski acts as postmistress.

More than 156,000 individual orders for First Day of Issue cancellations for the Crazy Horse stamp were processed in conjunction with the U.S. Post Office at Crazy Horse, which was established in 1968. Another 226,000 First Day of Issue cancellation orders from large commercial dealers were processed in Washington, D.C.

Doctor of Arts
Fairfield University

Fired by an heroic vision of unprecedented proportions you have given the last twenty years of your life "to make the white man know the red man also had great heroes." Braving ridicule and contempt, resisting political lures and federal monies, working yourself and your family to complete the monument which commemorates Chief Crazy Horse, you combine in your dedication the ferocity of moral conviction with the compulsion of art. In the tradition of Praxiteles and Michaelangelo you depict the Warrior Chief on horseback, leading his people and suing for peace. And this Sioux warrior, whose tragic history parallels the Indian's fate, has so exercised your energies that you are willing to lose your own life in order to find it. The power of beauty has rarely compelled such magnificent self-sacrifice.

From your earliest years, moreover, you displayed a fascination for the immortality and permanence which art confers. Learning your craft painfully and skillfully in the shipyards of East Boston, you moved from wood to marble, showing a preference for immortals like Artur Schnabel, Ignacy Paderewski, and Noah Webster. The techniques you later learned on Mount Rushmore . . . while working on the presidential sculptures, have brought you finally to the granite of Crazy Horse Mountain. Here, before the eyes of the world, you live out your dream that will transform the 6,700 foot mountain into a gigantic work of art. Blasting away tons of rock, year after year, you pit yourself against the impervious stone, until you realize your grand project, which will surely place you among the immortal sculptors of all times.

We are happy today recognizing your greatness; for we acknowledge this triumph of the human spirit: it enables man to take possession of the land and to dominate the forces of nature. Above all, we believe in the power of your imagination and moral passion.

In recognition of his merits, we the President and Trustees of Fairfield University do hereby create and proclaim

KORCZAK ZIOLKOWSKI

Doctor of Arts, honoris causa.

William C. McInnes, S.J.
President
Fairfield University
Fairfield, Connecticut
June 7, 1970

Doctor of Humane Letters
Black Hills State College

It is with both pride and pleasure that Black Hills State College today bestows the degree of Honorary Doctor of Humane Letters, Honoris Causa, on Korczak Ziolkowski — a man whose mark will be felt by civilization in the centuries ahead.

Korczak, this honor is not given to you only because of the massive mountain carving known as Crazy Horse. Rather, the faculty and administration of Black Hills State College have selected you for this honor because of your unselfish efforts in behalf of the human race and particularly in behalf of the North American Indian. Also, it is awarded because you have not been afraid to dream magnificent dreams — to assault a mountain and to leave to humanity a giant memory carved in granite and a more significant monument carved in love. I refer to your generous Indian scholarship program, your unequaled museum and your plans for a University and Medical Training Center devoted to Indian education and health care.

In your lifetime, you have received many honors — your marble portrait of Paderewski won first prize at the 1939 World's Fair; you received the Trustees Award of the National Cowboy Hall of Fame; you hold an Honorary Doctor of Fine Arts from Fairfield, Connecticut University; you are a member of the prestigious National Sculpture Society; your name is known to the international press — but the highest honor is that so many call you "friend" because you have given of yourself. Your friends come from many races, nationalities and walks of life and that list is headed by Black Hills State College's late President, Russell E. Jonas, and his wife, Lorena, who is here today.

We are not honoring a mountain masterpiece, nor are we honoring prized artwork or even a museum or scholarship program. Today, we are honoring you, Korczak Ziolkowski, the man whose mind conceived all of these giant works and whose heart transformed that impossible dream into a colossal reality for the benefit of all of humanity. We are honored that you have agreed to share today with us and to receive this award.

Dr. J. Gilbert Hause
President
Black Hills State College
Spearfish, South Dakota
May 15, 1981

Fifty-Eighth South Dakota Legislature
House Concurrent Resolution No. 1011

Introduced by: Representative Walter Dale Miller

Co-sponsored by Representatives Richard Hagen and Ron Volesky and Senators Don Frankenfeld and Thomas Shortbull

A CONCURRENT RESOLUTION, Commemorating Sculptor KORCZAK ZIOLKOWSKI, Storyteller in Stone, his legacy to the world and especially to the people of South Dakota, and designating May 3rd as KORCZAK ZIOLKOWSKI Day in South Dakota.

WHEREAS, old Sioux Indian chiefs invited KORCZAK to the Black Hills to carve a mountain memorial to their Chief Crazy Horse "so the white man would know the red man had great heroes, too"; and

WHEREAS, the truth, beauty and justice of their eloquent request inspired KORCZAK; and

WHEREAS, he arrived in the Black Hills on May 3, 1947, to begin the largest sculptural undertaking the world has ever known; and

WHEREAS, he promised the old Indian chiefs that Crazy Horse would be more than a mountain carving — it would be a humanitarian project, to include the Indian Museum of North America and the University and Medical Training Center for the North American Indian; and

WHEREAS, despite injuries, illnesses and advancing age he dedicated his life to fulfilling those promises; and

WHEREAS, in spite of severe financial hardship he rejected potential government funding for Crazy Horse, relying instead on the free enterprise system, in which he believed so strongly, to finance his work; and

WHEREAS, KORCZAK'S enormous progress on the colossal mountain carving and on the cultural and educational aspects of his project, exemplified the work ethic that made America great; and

WHEREAS, his efforts attracted international media attention, resulting in an incalculable contribution to South Dakota's tourism industry; and

WHEREAS, KORCZAK was born in Boston of Polish descent on September 6, 1908; and

WHEREAS, he was a patriotic American who proudly served his country in the Second World War, for which he volunteered at age 34, and in which he was seriously wounded twice; and

WHEREAS, he will be remembered not only for Crazy Horse but also for many other extraordinary works of sculpture for which he received numerous honors; and

WHEREAS, KORCZAK'S unselfish labors were dedicated to the noble conviction that every race must aspire to its greatest potential; and

WHEREAS, his life and vision inspired the lives of people everywhere; and

WHEREAS, realizing his project was larger than any one man's lifetime, he made detailed plans for the posthumous completion of Crazy Horse Memorial; and

WHEREAS, KORCZAK'S dream continues under the capable guidance of his wife, Ruth, and their large family; and

WHEREAS, in the seventy-fifth year of his life KORCZAK was laid to rest near the base of Thunderhead Mountain; and

WHEREAS, although the physical presence of the sculptor has left his mountain, his spirit remains; and

WHEREAS, KORCZAK'S mark will be felt by civilizations in future centuries:

NOW, THEREFORE, BE IT RESOLVED, by the House of Representatives of the Fifty-eighth Legislature of the state of South Dakota, the Senate concurring therein, that Sculptor KORCZAK ZIOLKOWSKI, Storyteller in Stone, be remembered for the legacy he left the world, especially the people of South Dakota, and that May 3rd be designated KORCZAK ZIOLKOWSKI Day in South Dakota.

Adopted by the House of Representatives,   February 8, 1983
Concurred in by the Senate,   February 8, 1983

A Tribute by Carl Levin

"Congressional Record"
United States Senate
December 2, 1982

MR. LEVIN: Mr. President, on October 20, 1982, a monumental American, Korczak Ziolkowski, died at his beloved Crazy Horse in the Black Hills of South Dakota. He was one of those rare people who changed the face of the planet and touched the souls of its inhabitants.

For over 35 years, he blasted away at a mountain to turn it into a monument to Chief Crazy Horse, based on his belief that native American heroes should be memorialized with the same grandeur and in the same spirit as later arriving heroes, such as those chiseled in the stone of Mount Rushmore.

Korczak worked on Mount Rushmore and was already a famous and accomplished sculptor when he decided, upon his return from World War II, to devote his life to transforming Thunderhead Mountain in South Dakota into a monument to Chief Crazy Horse. For three and one-half decades he blasted away millions of tons off the mountain, much of that time working alone. Supporting him below and later on the mountain itself were his extraordinary wife, Ruth, and their 10 children. Ruth and their large family are dedicated to carrying on Korczak's work according to his plans.

A number of years ago, I became fascinated with this wonderful man and came to know him, Ruth, and the children. I urged the U.S. Postal Service to issue a stamp in Crazy Horse's memory so that we could honor both the subject and the sculptor of the Crazy Horse Monument. The Postal Service and the country came through, and on September 6, 1981, we unveiled the design of the regular issue 13-cent Crazy Horse stamp at the Indian Museum of North America at Crazy Horse adjacent to Korczak's studio-home and looking out on his life's work.

My remarks at that time reflect my feelings about Korczak as well as Crazy Horse, and I repeat them now as part of this farewell to Korczak:

America is proud of a native son today. The legacy of Crazy Horse and the Native American heroes he symbolizes will be shared by millions as a result of the stamp and the design we unveil today.

As important as is the Crazy Horse legacy, a dual purpose prompted me to suggest that the Postal Service print this stamp.

The second purpose is the legacy of Korczak Ziolkowski. Oh, I know the rules of the Postal Service and they are right. And I know Korczak's rule—it is Crazy Horse that should be honored, not Korczak's monument to Crazy Horse.

But I know my own feelings, too, and I hope Korczak will understand. Perhaps never before (and perhaps never again) has there been such a physical and spiritual commitment of artist to subject. So while this stamp will memorialize Crazy Horse, it was inspired by Korczak's monument to Crazy Horse and by the spirituality of Korczak's mountain.

Imbued in that mountain is love and respect and redemption and celebration and proportion and wisdom.

We are enobled by Crazy Horse's life and Korczak's transcendent vision of it.

We are better people because we remember Crazy Horse today and because Korczak remembered him all these years.

And to Ruth and the family, who have made so much possible, and to Korczak's and Ruth's extraordinary circle of friends: your devotion to Korczak and his ideals is one of the noblest chapters in the story of how a God-like mountain has emerged to watch over this place.

The stamp itself was issued at Crazy Horse in the Black Hills on January 15, 1982. I wrote a poem for the occasion with which I would like to close this tribute:

POEM

The transcendent promise of America both
    to her native people and
    to newcomers,
That we can be one with each other
    and with the land
Is being redeemed on Crazy Horse
    Mountain.
That mountain's sculptor, Korczak, has
    received two gifts from God,
Creative power and an enduring devotion
    to the ideal of brotherhood.
Korczak's gift in return is to we mortals
    and to immortality.
The mountain on whose crest a great
    chief slowly wakes
Was lonely witness to the marriage of the
    Spirits of Crazy Horse and Korczak,
While Korczak's wife and children brought
    succor and in late epochs
Shared in the dynamite's blast.
With each blast's roar we are redeemed.
With each blast's song we are uplifted.
With each blast's hymn the Godlike mountain
    emerges and our spirits soar.
With each blast, Crazy Horse Mountain,
    Korczak's mountain, looks more like it
    was envisioned to be,
When, a lifetime ago, Korczak said yes.
Now, a lifetime hence, his unstilled yes
Transforms his mountain and our souls.

—Carl Levin

Eulogy by Robert Fast Horse

At Memorial Services For
Sculptor Korczak Ziolkowski
Crazy Horse Memorial
October 24, 1982

This is an especially difficult task, for me to speak today. I, too, have lost this past year, lost my grandfather and father. I know the confusion and sadness that's in your heart at this time about death. I've often contemplated the death of our people and the reason why. I was listening to the songs and prayers that were offered this afternoon, and they moved my spirit.

The name that was given to Mr. Ziolkowski, Shooting Star, was like a meteorite, it marks an event in time, the gift of a newborn infant or the passing of an elder. It was almost 44 years ago that Chief Henry Standing Bear approached Korczak. He said, "My fellow Chiefs and I would like the White Man to know the Red Man had great heroes, too." And, there is its beginning, carved into the mountainside. A truth will be established.

It must be said today that two races of people have lost a great man. At a time when it was fashionable for racial hatred, he obeyed God's Commandment. In the English language it is: love one another. He's a man who dared to be different. He dared to cross the artificial barriers, and for this we respect him. It is for this reason our hearts lie on the ground.

Because we understand your loss let it be said today also that this image of a great man, Crazy Horse, is matched by a great inspiration of a man who had a great heart, Korczak Ziolkowski. I was reading some of the signs that have his name. I would like to request that these signs stay the same, that the signs don't change. As his spirit will continue to live. Crazy Horse Monument was a great vision, the establishment of the Museum, the planned University and Medical Training Center, a Memorial fund for Indian people, especially at a time when our people remain impoverished.

A lot of us have held a great esteem for this project, for this figure of Crazy Horse. It gives us pride to think of Crazy Horse, to think that his image is going to last. Although we seem to be in a mobile age, at a time when our people are downtrodden, we can look at this man, Crazy Horse, and thank the man who's done it.

We can be a proud people because of this. Let it be said that this shrine represents the freedom, the nation of Indian people. Thank you.

Eulogy by Father William O'Connell

At Memorial Services For
Sculptor Korczak Ziolkowski
Crazy Horse Memorial
October 24, 1982

A CELEBRATION OF LIFE — A TRIBUTE

Legends, dreams, visions, greatness — this beautiful fall afternoon, as we come to offer the gift of our presence to Ruth and her children, as we come to pay our final respects to a remarkable man — this is what we come to celebrate — legends, dreams, visions and greatness — and their embodiment in the life and work of our dear friend, Korczak.

We can never forget that above all Korczak was a man! And in so many things just like us — enjoying a good laugh, savoring a fine drink, cherishing a true friendship. And like us — angered at incompetence, proud of accomplishments, ready to fight for ideals. And unlike so many of us a man who grubbed existence from the earth, hammered away at its riches, chiseled at its mountains — yet capable, in a most unusual way, of flying into the highest heavens with his articulate reasonings.

This afternoon there are some personal reflections I would like to share with you — in hopes that these will put legends, dreams, visions and greatness into proper perspective.

All of us are aware of the hard, burdensome path Korczak trod for 74 years. Orphaned at one, physically abused by foster parents as infant and child, encouraged to develop his talents by a most perceptive judge, becoming an internationally acclaimed sculptor, wading through the bloodied beaches of Normandy, accepting the challenge of Thunderhead Mountain — and in the 35 long years that followed tossing off illnesses and surgeries that would have destroyed a lesser person.

Indeed, in honesty, I feel that many of us would have cried "enough is enough" early on. Others would have blamed the environment of early childhood for their lack of ability, their insecurity. But Korczak didn't.

And I firmly believe that he did not because he was a virtuous man. Not in the virtue of a plaster saint adorning a church wall. St. Thomas Aquinas teaches that virtues are acquired strengths, attained through determined discipline. Korczak possessed such strengths.

In his first letter as Pope, a fellow Pole, Karol Woytja, Pope John Paul II addressed the human condition. He who had worked in the quarries near Krakow, who had suffered the idignities of Nazi repression, who lived so long under Communist oppression spoke about the dignity inherent in each of us —

and how we were able to bring this dignity to full stature through the acquired strengths, the virtues attained through discipline. In so many ways Korczak mirrored the image drawn in Redemptor Hominus.

There are many virtues we could speak about: perseverance, long-suffering, faithfulness. There is one I would like to stress. The strength of being a family man.

Undoubtedly you have seen the video tapes where, almost tongue in cheek, Korczak says he told Ruth the mountain came first, she second, and the children third. In the immensity of his love for family there were no such priorities.

Certainly Korczak was a hard father. But I believe this came from what he had suffered without a family of his own to grow up in. He wanted to have the best of families — demanding from each almost the perfection he demanded of good stone for his work. Despite his gruffness, his impatience, underneath was a love greater than he was able to show, or the family was ever able to experience. His greatest strength was in his love for that which constituted his family — Ruth, the children and the mountain. Anyone who spoke anything against any portion of this, his family, would know his wrath. Here (with his family) and there (on the mountain) is his greatest strength — his virtue.

We all know what a visionary Korczak was. You could not set out to carve a mountain without being one.

Unlike those who see things as they are and say why, he looked and saw things as they could be and said, why not. It is his "why not?" that has brought us here today.

What of the visionary marriage of Korczak and Crazy Horse? Initially this was not a romantic, idealistic union. It was a post-war job, that became the challenge of a life time. Korczak did not come West motivated by an overwhelming love for the Indian people, nor, at that time, by a deep understanding of their culture. He came to work on a mountain sculpture. He stayed to live a love-affair.

For soon, quite soon, he became aware that he was about more than a mountain carving. He was using his remarkable talents to champion a people whose heroes were looked down upon — whose culture, whose way of life was being ground in the grist mill of material prosperity.

As he studied about Crazy Horse, as he read the wise words of so many of the chiefs and elders — they spoke to his heart, they transformed his spirit. They contained so much of the same common sense as he found in Aristotle's treatise "On Nature."

The love affair began. The vision was that the world must know more of a man, who at age 33, gave his life for his people; that the example of Crazy Horse was a faithful model for all peoples.

It was this love that enabled Korczak to spend 35 years of difficult toil — to literally give his life for this same man, and for his people.

Looking out we can see the arduous task ahead to complete this epic dream — to fulfill this vision.

To do honor to our friend, on this day, at this time, we must ask — where are we in the completion of the dream? What is our role in the fulfillment of this vision — so that greatness can live on?

It is incumbent upon all of us who have been touched by Korczak's spirit, who have glimpsed the potential of that dream of mountain, university and medical training center and Indian Museum — to pledge ourselves this day before this mountain and this man to see to its fulfillment. It will not be finished in the lifetimes of many of us — but let us promise now that we will do all we can to see that it is completed — so help us God.

But there is one more point to the story of Crazy Horse, the epic sculpture in stone. How often we who were privileged to be Korczak's friends, heard him speak — almost in a sense of hushed awe of the culture and heroes of the Indian people.

In the last conversation I had with him he said, "Next year, when I'm feeling better, I will speak out more forcefully for the Indian people. I want everyone to know the beauty of their lives. The gifts they gave us. The justness of their cause."

Death snatched that opportunity from Korczak — but circumstances have given it to us.

On this most solemn day let us pledge ourselves to a deeper understanding of the beauty of Indian culture, the Indian way — to a healing of mind and soul and spirit so that this monument will not merely be a symbol of Indian greatness, but so that Korczak's work will be a symbol of the full acceptance we each must have for one another — as brothers and sisters whose time for walking this path of life is, oh, so short.

When legends die, dreams cease. When dreams cease there is no greatness. Korczak Ziolkowski has given us a legend, a dream, a greatness.

His part of the storytelling is finished. Ours has just begun. May we be blessed to use our talents as well as he did. And may God, our Eternal Father, grant this loving husband, dedicated father, this powerhouse of talent, the fullness of Eternal Glory. AMEN.

Resolution Of The Oglala Sioux Tribe
Executive Committee

RESOLUTION COMMEMORATING THE DEATH OF KORCZAK ZIOLKOWSKI, SCULPTOR OF CRAZY HORSE MEMORIAL.

WHEREAS, Korczak Ziolkowski, the famed sculptor of the Crazy Horse Memorial has devoted and dedicated 35 years of his life carving the Crazy Horse Memorial in honor of Oglala War Chief Crazy Horse, and

WHEREAS, the Oglala Lakota Nation had great admiration and respect for Mr. Ziolkowski, and

WHEREAS, on October 20th, 1982, Mr. Ziolkowski died and the Oglala Sioux people now greatly mourn his passing, now

THEREFORE BE IT RESOLVED, that the Oglala Sioux Tribe hereby commemorates the death of Mr. Korczak Ziolkowski and directs the Oglala Sioux Tribe to express the condolences of the Oglala Sioux people to Mrs. Ruth Ziolkowski's family, and present a tribal flag to Mr. Ziolkowski's widow as a tribute and honor for dedicating 35 years of his life carving the Crazy Horse Memorial in honor of Oglala War Chief Crazy Horse and all Lakota people.

October 26, 1982
Pine Ridge, S.D.

Resolution Of The Rosebud Sioux Tribe
Tribal Council

WHEREAS, The Rosebud Sioux Tribe is a federally recognized Tribe organized pursuant to the Indian Reorganization Act of 1934 and all pertinent amendments thereof, and

WHEREAS, Sculptor Korczak Ziolkowski dedicated his life to carving a monument to honor the memory of Crazy Horse, a recognized and honored Lakota leader, and

WHEREAS, The Crazy Horse Monument was undertaken as a humanitarian project to honor all American Indians, and

WHEREAS, The Rosebud Sioux Tribe recognized that the mother of Crazy Horse was a Sicangu Lakota and a sister of Chief Spotted Tail, and

WHEREAS, The Rosebud Sioux Tribe desires to support the completion of the Crazy Horse Monument, now

THEREFORE BE IT RESOLVED, that the Rosebud Sioux Tribe, through its elected Tribal Council and Officers, does hereby endorse and pledge its support to the completion of the Crazy Horse Monument by the Board of Directors of the Crazy Horse Memorial Foundation.

November 1, 1982
Rosebud, S.D.

Standing Rock Sioux Tribe

Dear Mrs. Ziolkowski and Family:

On behalf of the Standing Rock Sioux Tribe, I would like to extend our deepest heartfelt sympathy in the recent death of your husband and father, Korczak.

Although he is gone from this life, we share and are consoled by the dream he had, by his lifetime project, the Crazy Horse Memorial, being sculpted in the Black Hills, a most sacred place for all Native Americans, especially the Sioux. The knowledge that his work will go on and will be completed strengthens all of us, and the dedication and determination shown by Korczak will exemplify what we strive for in our struggle to retain our own identity and sovereignty.

Again, on behalf of all of the members of the Standing Rock Sioux Tribe, we extend our sincere sympathy at his passing, and look forward to the completion of the Crazy Horse Memorial.

Sincerely,
Charles Murphy, Vice Chairman

Standing Rock Sioux Tribe
Ft. Yates, N.D.

65

"Every Man Has His Mountain— I'm Carving Mine."

(Editor's note: The following representative excerpts are drawn from the more than 6,000 cards and letters Mrs. Ziolkowski and her family received following Korczak's death October 20, 1982. The letters bring to mind Korczak's often stated belief every person should strive to give back something, to try to leave the world a little better place.)

He was larger than life, and he's larger than death, too. He became part of me . . . of how many, I wonder?

New York, N.Y.

He was not an ordinary man to tackle a mountain . . . He was a very big man for his word and loyalty alone.

What some men might say of a promise made to an Indian 40 years or so before as being heedless, Korczak said it was his word to an old Indian and it had to do with what is right.

He and his family worked on the mountain for years and years through hard times and better times, and what it boils down to is that it was a work pursued toward the realization of the Indian legend and the Indian dignity . . .

He was the man who was as big as his mountain . . . He was a big man for his devotion, as a humanitarian and certainly as an artist.

Fresno, California

. . . Korczak had a profound effect on me. He represents a Spirit of America; a force that believed in a cause, an independence, and had the determination to maintain that force to the end . . . He was frustrated by a body that would not do what he asked of it. Pain was part of his existence, but weakness was not . . .

Covered with rock dust, running a bulldozer, hanging from the side of the mountain, carving for the Indians; putting his life into an ideal for this country; he achieved a greatness that few men will ever know.

Farmington, Connecticut

. . . This is not a sympathy card—it is a thank you . . . most of all, for the knowledge that, in this world of compromise and failing, one man—and one woman— can have and keep a dream, and live accordingly.

Oregon

He was a good man. You should be *very* proud. I don't even have a job, but I do have this $10. Please use it for the mountain. When I get on my economic feet again, I'll send some more.

Huntington, West Virginia

. . . Last summer we visited Crazy Horse Mt., and I can't tell you the feeling it gave me. I'll never forget that feeling. Never. I had tears in my eyes . . .

Crazy Horse will be completed; it already has the heartbeat.

El Paso, Texas

. . . His light will shine in my life because of what he did; he lived for something greater than himself.

Shawnee, Oklahoma

KORCZAK
A dream was born—died—and yet
is still alive
Because this man's goal will
circumvent death.
Out of the mountain, Crazy Horse
in time will arrive
Symbolizing for all mankind—
what his people have left.
Korczak's monument will point forever;
the word is carried
"My lands are where my dead lie buried."

Plattsburgh, N.Y.

. . . Korczak was one of the giants of my lifetime . . . whose work and vision will remain always with the people whose lives he touched and inspired.

When I was a 16-year-old kid in Sacramento, California, and even long before that, he was at work on his mountain. He was there through most of my life. And,

"Never forget your dreams" was Korczak's message to the 1981 graduating class of Black Hills State College, whose President, Dr. J. Gilbert Hause, bestowed on the sculptor an honorary Doctorate of Humane Letters. It was only the tenth honorary doctorate awarded in the college's nearly 100-year history. Korczak never had the opportunity to attend college, and he never took a lesson in art, sculpture, engineering or architecture.

he represented a thread of enduring continuity in a life of change, something as solid as the mountains and the Earth itself, on which I could always depend.

He helped make me strong when I needed to be. When one looks for some genuine verities and eternities to believe in, one looks for men like Korczak Ziolkowski.

Knowing he was there was knowing the pillars still stand, the stars are where they belong, the rivers still run.

Few men have had as great a dream as Korczak Ziolkowski, or as great a dedication. I never met him, and never saw his work except in photos, but I loved the man, loved his commitment, loved what he was doing.

Korczak Ziolkowski was one of the true heroes of the 20th century, and I will treasure always the memories, the meanings, the collection of articles and photos . . . and that mountain in South Dakota.

Merritt Island, Florida

. . . For the common person of the world, I say, "thank you."

I sincerely hope that Crazy Horse will be completed. What a beautiful monument . . .   Ramsey, New Jersey

. . . It is difficult to measure the stature of Korczak because he stands alone. He is unique . . . If he had been granted time to finish his project, posterity would have ranked him with Leonardo da Vinci and Michelangelo.

Korczak was so ordinary in manner, so full of fun and laughter, we people in western South Dakota did not realize his stature or his astonishing abilities, did not realize that we were living with genius of a degree which shows up once in half a thousand years.   Pine Ridge, S.D.

We want to express our heartfelt thanks to the Ziolkowski family for their courage in carrying on Korczak's work. We know this plan was pre-ordained.

Losing Korczak is sad, but losing his dream would have been tragic.

Charlevois, Michigan

. . . It is an age-old tradition among the Pueblo Indians here in the Southwest to provide all men who have departed this world with a water jug so that they may have water and not thirst on their journey to the other world. Traditionally the vessel is filled with water and broken on the ground at the place of burial; however, we are sending this water jug as a symbolic gift which you may use in the traditional way, or keep it intact as an honor to Korczak; the choice is yours . . . He was a very, very great man.

Checotah, Oklahoma

(Editor's note: The water jug—filled with liquid—was placed in Korczak's tomb near the base of the mountain carving.)

. . . I will remember him, not only for his great artistry, but his strength to correct things that were wrong . . .

Livingston, Montana

. . . Although I never met him, I feel a sense of personal loss. Korczak was one of my heroes . . .

You already will have received tributes to the life and work of Korczak far better expressed than anything I could pen. What I can say is that, if ever a life was worth having, it was that of Korczak Ziolkowski . . .

He had life and he had it abundantly and he lived to the full; he had the invaluable bonus of the support of his family . . .

Chichester, England

. . . The tribute given Korczak and his life's work by Dan Rather on the CBS-TV "Evening News" is well-deserved recognition of his selfless perseverance through the years . . .

Muskogee, Oklahoma

. . . I have just returned from a lengthy overseas business trip, and at the time I heard of Korczak's death, my wife and I were in France where the news was published. The fact that Korczak and his work has world renown is perhaps of some comfort to you and your family.

We all have suffered a loss—the ambitions and inspirations of a great artist—Korczak.

Denver, Colorado

. . . I was very moved by the power and emotion in Korczak's sculptures. I cannot adequately describe the feelings except to say that Korczak's works touched something in my soul.

DePere, Wisconsin

In 1981 we were pleased to visit Crazy Horse. We had been traveling through many states and visited many memorials, etc. with so many contributions required that when we came to your gate we both thought maybe we should bypass this one, but said, "oh, well, this may be different."

It was the best five dollars we spent in our 26-state trip. Our only regret was we didn't have more time to spend at your wonderful monument. Everyone was so nice. If we are fortunate enough to make such a trip again, we will again visit you.

We were sorry to hear of Korczak's passing. Please keep up his work—for which we enclose this small contribution.

Sanger, California

. . . I never met him, but I know Korczak was a tough man. It was his kind that made this country. And, as long as that kind of person is around, we always will be a kind country.

Montrose, S.D.

. . . We shall miss him even more the more we contemplate all his sculpture.

His advice that "you must work on the mountain—but slowly, so you do it right," is wonderful advice. Slowly. So you do it right.

Luverne, Minnesota

. . . Korczak has left the legacy not only of his art—but the examples of his life.

Our Black Hills have been exceptionally blessed with men like Korczak Ziolkowski and Gutzon Borglum—men with spirit and strength, determination and daring, and with the vision to see not what is, but what might be. Thank you.

Rapid City, S.D.

Through his energies and his insights he has enlightened mankind and made the world a somewhat better place and more worthwhile to live in . . .

San Angelno, California

THE WHITE HOUSE

WASHINGTON

November 1, 1982

Dear Mrs. Ziolkowski:

Nancy and I want to express our heartfelt condolences to you and to your family on Mr. Ziolkowski's death.

I know there are no words which will make your burden easier to bear, but I hope that your spirits are sustained by the warm memories Mr. Ziolkowski has left behind and through the many prayers being said for you during these sad days.

Your husband's vision and dream for a memorial in honor of the American Indian inspire all who reach and who achieve with spirit and determination. He was a man of considerable accomplishment, and you can take great pride in him.

God bless and keep you always.

Sincerely,

Ronald Reagan

. . . It is a wonder to me how a person in such discomfort and pain could keep his dream alive and his talents working. A genius is a person with the ability to discipline oneself to work hard and long to develop and use God-given talents. That was Korczak—he was big and did big things in a big way. Thank God he had his thin spots—so we can realize he was human.

Surry, Maine

. . . Korczak's life's work must remain a role model for all idealistic youth of today . . .

Hartford, Connecticut

. . . Korczak reminded us that greatness comes only from vision and the sweat of the brow. Let us hope that our nation will, inspired by Korczak, learn this lesson. As Shakespeare said it: "To thine own self be true, and it must follow as the night the day, Thou then cannot be false to any man."

Washington, D.C.

Eventually Korczak's heroic figure of an American Indian on horseback will be outlined against the sky. Like the pyramids of Egypt, it will stand for all time to come, at least a thousand years and a day . . .

Hastings, Iowa

. . . On seeing the postcard of the "Future of Crazy Horse," I am reminded of the tomb of Christopher Wren, designer-builder of the magnificent St. Paul's Cathedral in London. It is but a plain tomb amongst beautiful ones of famous men in the crypt of the cathedral. It simply says on it, "If you seek a monument, look around you." There is a parallel here with Korczak. His marvelous achievements will be for all to see.

May I wish you continuing success in continuing the work already well on its way to completion.

Nottinghamshire, England

. . . I am proud to be one of the Sioux Indians the great artist was honoring. I am grateful to him . . .

Apple Valley, California

Korczak touched my life . . . I have two favorite "Korczak musings." One is: "When the legends die, the dreams end; when the dreams end, there is no more greatness." The other is: "The world asks you one question: did you do your job? The answer is not: I would have done it if people had been nicer . . . if I'd had the money . . . if I hadn't died; if's don't count. The answer must be: yes!"

Pierre, South Dakota

. . . The man changed me fundamentally . . . I can tell you how I feel. I remember reading once about a baseball fan who had just been told that Babe Ruth had died. "I know," he said. "But I don't have to believe it if I don't want to."

Las Vegas, Nevada

Pope John Paul Accepts Korczak's Bronze Crazy Horse Scale Model

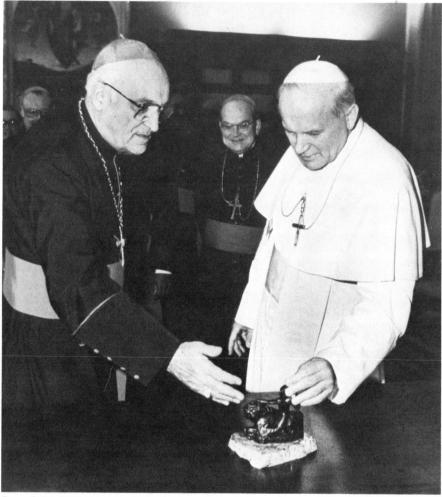

Pope John Paul II admires the bronze cast of Korczak's small Crazy Horse model.

Pope John Paul II enthusiastically accepted a bronze cast of Korczak's 1/1,200th scale model for his Crazy Horse mountain carving, now in progress in the Black Hills of South Dakota.

The presentation was made at the Vatican in December, 1983, on behalf of Mrs. Ziolkowski by the Most Reverend Harold J. Dimmerling, Bishop of the Diocese of Rapid City, S.D. He said, "The Pope was extremely pleased with the Crazy Horse bronze. He examined and scrutinized it very carefully."

Mrs. Ziolkowski said, "Korczak would have been greatly honored and humbled by the Pope's acceptance of his work. Korczak had the greatest admiration for Pope John Paul's religious and political struggles in Poland before he was elected Pontiff. Although he always said he was an American, Korczak also was proud of his Polish ancestry."

I'm Glad There Was A Korczak Ziolkowski

(Editor's note: Korczak's passing brought tributes in many forms from throughout the United States and many foreign countries. High among the Ziolkowski family's favorites is the following by Bob Colver, editorial writer for the *Charlotte* (N.C.) *News*.)

I am going to miss Korczak Ziolkowski. He died last week at the age of 74. I never met him. I've never ever seen his mountain. But I don't like to think of the world running out of Korczak Ziolkowskis.

Korczak Ziolkowski was a sculptor. In a big way was Korczak Ziolkowski a sculptor. He spent the last 34 years of his life working on one statue. And it is still not finished.

In 1948, Korczak Ziolkowski dynamited 10 tons of granite from the side of Thunderhead Mountain near Custer, S.D. It was the ceremonial first chip of his statue of the great Sioux chief Crazy Horse.

When Mr. Ziolkowski's dream is completed—and his wife and 10 children say it *will* be completed—Thunderhead Mountain will become the world's largest statue. Crazy Horse, seated on his war pony, his arm pointing out across the Black Hills, will be 563 feet high and 641 feet long. Four thousand people would be able to stand on the outstretched arm. A 10-story building would fit in between the arm and the horse's neck, and the eyeball of the horse will be two stories tall.

It takes a certain kind of vision to look at a mountain and see a statue. It takes a certain kind of brass to presume that what you are going to do with that mountain is going to be an improvement. And it takes a certain kind of determination.

Korczak Ziolkowski was two months shy of 40 when he started on Thunderhead Mountain. A few years ago, when he turned 70, he recognized that it would probably take another 20 years to complete—maybe longer. He knew his heart, or the mountain, would probably kill him before he could look upon a finished Crazy Horse. But he kept climbing up on the mountain, blasting away with his dynamite and chiseling away with his jackhammer and his bulldozer.

His heart finally got him. His last words to his wife were: "Crazy Horse must be finished. You must work on the mountain—but slowly, so you do it right."

Korczak Ziolkowski's vision was a bold one, an epic one, perhaps a vain one. But it was a uniquely American vision.

There is something in the air or the water or something in this country that inspires people like Korczak Ziolkowski to undertake to leave their mark on the land and leave it in a big way. And it may be only coincidence that most of them were immigrants or, like Mr. Ziolkowski, children of immigrants.

Gutzon Borglum was an Idaho-born son of Danish immigrants. He was a classically trained artist. His was the first piece of American sculpture bought for the Metropolitan Museum in New York. His output—both in quantity and quality—would have satisfied most artists. But Gutzon Borglum was not going to be content until he had left something behind on the land. Like Korczak Ziolkowski, he picked a mountain in South Dakota. His was called Mount Rushmore.

Constantino Brumidi fled his native Italy in 1852 and landed in New York. He, too, had a classical art background and had painted frescoes in the Vatican. But in 1855, he started his masterpiece—the United States Capitol.

It began with a mural in the Agriculture Committee room. From then until his death in 1880, he painted. He painted the canopy of the Rotunda. He painted portraits and thousands of frescoes. He literally covered the interior of the Capitol with paintings, including intricate paintings of American birds and plants in obscure corridors only the guards and janitors know about. He did it, he said, to repay America for being there when he needed it.

Simon Rodia wanted to say "thank you," too. Simon Rodia, however, did not have an artistic background. And there are some that say his towers in the Watts section of Los Angeles show it. Mr. Rodia worked in concrete. And in anything else he could find to imbed in his concrete— seashells, broken glass, horseshoes, rocks, broken pottery. With those materials, he created eight towers spread over a square block of Watts. Sometimes lacy, sometimes tangled, they look from a distance like some kind of bizarre radio antennae or a set from a 1950s science fiction movie.

Los Angeles is still arguing whether they are art or whether they are junk. But whatever they are, they are. And they are what Simon Rodia wanted them to be—his addition to the American landscape. "I was raised here, you understand?" he told an interviewer once. "I wanted to do something for the United States, because there are nice people in this country."

I wonder what makes a Korczak Ziol-kowski, a Gutzon Borglum, a Constantino Brumidi or a Simon Rodia tick. I wonder what makes them see their artistic visions in terms of acres and miles of corridors instead of square feet of canvas, in terms of mountains instead of blocks of marble.

It would be an interesting piece of research for some student looking for a Ph.D. or for a Ph.D. looking for a full professorship. Except they probably couldn't document it. It's not there on paper to be excerpted and footnoted.

But it is there in Watts, in Washington, on Mount Rushmore and, in a rough form, on Thunderhead Mountain.

I hope it continues to pop up from time to time.

—Bob Colver

... Inspired by His Life, Vision and Legacy

The 36th annual report (October 20, 1983) of the Crazy Horse Memorial Foundation includes the following paragraph, which opens the section about 1983's five stages of progress on the mountain carving:

"Resuming work on the mountain carving without Korczak was very difficult emotionally for Ruth and the Ziolkowski family. But,

... motivated by their individual and collective dedication to carry on Korczak's dream,

... supported by his great faith and confidence in them,

... schooled by his years of instruction,

... toughened by his example,

... uplifted by his sense of humor,

... guided by his detailed plans and scale models, and

... inspired by his life, vision and legacy, the Ziolkowski family began its chapter of progress on the Crazy Horse mountain carving Memorial Day, May 30, 1983. The first of four blasts set off that day was at 11:11 a.m. in the area above the horse's head near Korczak's first cut into the mountain."

The Foundation Board of Directors meeting opened with adoption of the following motion by Recording Secretary Mrs. Jessie Sundstrom of Custer, S.D.:

"Mr. President, it is with profound regret that today I move for the record that the death of Korczak Ziolkowski one year ago today on October 20, 1982, be acknowledged with the deepest gratitude of this Commission for the devotion of thirty-five years that he gave to the carving of Chief Crazy Horse and the planning of the humanitarian aspects of the project, for which he truly gave his life.

"I also move that the members of the Commission make a serious commit-ment today to carry on the work of Korczak's dream by helping his family and the Memorial in any way possible with generous sharing of time and talent in a manner emulating Korczak's devotion in a celebration of his life to our mutual benefit, and for the good of the American Indian and all mankind."

Corn Mural Pays Unusual Tribute to Korczak

This tapestry in corn was one of the most unusual tributes paid to Korczak. The eight-by-30-foot panel on the famous Mitchell, S.D., Corn Palace was completed September 6, 1983, Korczak's 75th birth date. It was created from various colored ears of corn—perhaps 1,000 in the Crazy Horse model and mountain and another 2,500 in the sky and adjoining side panels. The detail was achieved by using rows of corn as narrow as one kernel wide.

Korczak Receives Black Elk Award

Korczak has been honored posthumously by the South Dakota Tourism Department for his contributions to the state's travel industry. During the nearly 36 years he worked on Crazy Horse, the sculptor and his project attracted ongoing national and international publicity worth tens of millions of dollars to the state's tourism promotion efforts.

He was named the 1983 recipient of the Ben Black Elk Award "for excellence in tourism development." The inscription on the plaque accompanying the travelling trophy reads:

"To Korczak Ziolkowski for a lifetime in pursuit of a dream that is becoming reality and will one day be a legend."

The Ben Black Elk Award commemorates the man who personally greeted visitors at Mt. Rushmore National Memorial for over 27 years. Its presentation to Korczak brings a long friendship "full circle."

Shortly after Korczak arrived in the Black Hills in 1947 to begin the mountain carving at the request of old Sioux Indian Chiefs, the sculptor visited Ben's father, Old Black Elk. He was a cousin of Crazy Horse, a survivor of the Battle of Little Big Horn and a Holy Man. Old Black Elk was one of the men who knew Crazy Horse, who told Korczak that Crazy Horse had said, "I will come back to you in the stone."

About this same time, his son, Ben Black Elk, had suffered a great personal loss. His father sent the young man to visit Korczak and keep a vigil at the foot of Crazy Horse Mountain, where he camped for almost two weeks. He and Korczak developed a strong friendship, and members of the Black Elk family visited Crazy Horse often over the years. When Korczak entertained the National Press Photographers Association for a day at Crazy Horse, Ben Black Elk sang "The Song of Crazy Horse" for them from the top of the mountain carving.

February 5, 1982

Executive Proclamation
State of South Dakota
Office Of The Governor

WHEREAS, Henry Standing Bear, a Chief of the Oglala Sioux Indian Tribe, watched the white man sculpt Mount Rushmore into the sacred granite of a Paha Sapa mountain as a tribute and lasting memorial to the civilization of the white race; and,

WHEREAS, Henry Standing Bear in 1939 wrote to a Boston-born Polish sculptor who had just won The First Sculptural Award at The New York World's Fair for his bust of Paderewski, and asked that young sculptor to carve an heroic equestrian statue of the great Sioux, Crazy Horse, into the sacred granite of a Paha Sapa mountain as a tribute and lasting memorial to the civilization of the Red Race; and,

WHEREAS, The young sculptor, named Korczak Ziolkowski, was moved by the request and inspired by the truth, beauty and justice of the mission, accepted the commission, and took as his mandate the eloquent request of Chief Standing Bear to carve a statue that would depict the story of Indian Civilization at its zenith and "not left at the end of the trail which depicts the Indian in despair"; and,

WHEREAS, By Korczak Ziolkowski's epic work, the story of the American Indian in the full flower of his civilization shall never pass from the earth, but will belong forever to the ages; and,

WHEREAS, To allay Standing Bear's concern that the Indian would be remembered not at all or as a broken, defeated man, this noble, classical, epic statue will say to generations of ages yet to come, "I was here, on this land, and I was a magnificent man"; and,

WHEREAS, Korczak Ziolkowski carved the heritage of the Indian race upon the face of eternity, he, too, shall not pass from human experience, and as long as there is one human being left to cast his eyes upon "this magnificent man," the artistic compact will be realized; this sculpture will say again and again, to all who behold it, "I was here, on this land, and I was a magnificent man"; and,

WHEREAS, I shall not pass as Governor without honoring the man who in this colossal effort gave all of himself to all of humanity forever; this I cannot do; it would be too large an oversight; and,

WHEREAS, To commemorate our tribute to Korczak Ziolkowski, I have caused a medallion to be cast bearing testimony to the high esteem we have for him:

NOW, THEREFORE, I, WILLIAM JANKLOW, Governor of the State of South Dakota, do hereby proclaim

KORCZAK ZIOLKOWSKI

the sole recipient into posterity, of The Governor's Award For Capital Achievement In The Arts in order to render the just recognition to a premier artist of our age.

IN WITNESS THEREFORE, I have hereunto set my hand and caused to be affixed the Great Seal of the State of South Dakota, in Pierre, the Capital City, this Fifth Day of February, in the Year of Our Lord, Nineteen Hundred and Eighty-Two.

ALICE KUNDERT
Secretary of State

WILLIAM J. JANKLOW
Governor

Medallion Recognizes Korczak

The Korczak medallion was unveiled in 1984 by Mrs. Ruth Ziolkowski and daughters (from left) Jadwiga, Anne and Monique. The bronze measures 16" in diameter and weighs 60 pounds.

Crazy Horse Sculptor Korczak Ziolkowski has been honored on the first medallion ever created by the State of South Dakota for permanent display in the statehouse in Pierre.

Governor William Janklow said he had the medallion created in recognition of Korczak's unique contributions to South Dakota and the world.

At the unveiling of the 60-pound bronze in a February, 1984, ceremony in the capitol rotunda attended by the South Dakota Legislature, the Governor paid tribute to Korczak, saying, "This one-time-only medal recognizes achievement—achievement not in terms of what's been finished, but achievement in terms of what's being done on a magnitude the likes of which the world has never known.

"There are very few men or women who have ever lived who have utilized their talents and their God-given abilities as Korczak did to leave something of epic proportions for others following behind them. Not so they remember the individual as much as they remember what

the individual has left as a heritage, culture, appreciation or understanding," said Janklow. "The dream and creativity that Korczak brought to South Dakota with Crazy Horse lives on, not only on the mountain carving but on the equally important cultural and educational aspects of Crazy Horse."

Mrs. Korczak Ziolkowski attended the unveiling to express her appreciation to the governor on behalf of Korczak and their family. She said, "Korczak knew about this medallion because it was two years ago this month that Governor Janklow's beautiful Executive Proclamation creating the medal was brought to him at Crazy Horse. He was very touched by it, and I know Korczak would be pleased with this wonderful bronze bas-relief. I'd like to assure you all, South Dakotans and Americans who care, that the family and I intend to spend the rest of our lives—and we're more determined than ever—carrying on Korczak's dreams and making them become the reality for which he worked so hard."

American Polish Engineering Association Honors Korczak

The American Polish Engineering Association has posthumously honored Sculptor Korczak Ziolkowski with its prestigious Achievement Award.

At formal ceremonies in Detroit, Michigan, in February, 1984, the sculptor's daughter, Jadwiga, accepted the high award on behalf of her father.

Korczak was honored as a self-taught sculptor, engineer and architect for his "magnificent project of carving a Memorial to the Indians of North America out of a mountain in the Black Hills of South Dakota."

The President of the American Polish Engineering Association, Edward Cisak, who is the Industrial-Engineering Manager of Ford Motor Company at Wixom, Michigan, praised Korczak for the many and varying engineering achievements he accomplished in his nearly 36 years of work on Crazy Horse. He also lauded the sculptor for the foresight he showed in the comprehensive plans he left for the continuation of the mountain carving and for the fulfillment of the cultural and educational aspects of his Crazy Horse Memorial humanitarian project.

Cisak also read a letter from Michigan Senator Carl Levin, who was responsible for the creation and issuance of the 13¢ Crazy Horse U.S. postage stamp. Senator Levin said, in part, "I have been a long-time admirer of Korczak Ziolkowski and his work. His outstanding talent, dedication and determination will live forever in the Black Hills of South Dakota. I add my voice of tribute and ask Jadwiga to take back with her my best wishes to the family of Korczak, whose support made it possible for Korczak to fulfill his extraordinary vision."

Resolution Of The Akwesasne Six Nations Indian Museum
Onchiota, New York
October, 1982

WHEREAS, Sakoiatison, our Creator - The Great Spirit, has seen fit to take from this life our esteemed friend, brother, and fellow worker among our people, BRAVE WOLF (KORCZAK ZIOLKOWSKI), and

WHEREAS, his passing is indeed an inestimable loss to all of us as a race, and we realize thereby that another of our GREAT who has many, many times brought honour to his Indian People, and of whom we are all proud, has taken the Sunset Trail. His passing is a loss to America and especially to Indian Peoples.

As a carver, a sculptor and a champion of Indian Peoples of America, the Great Spirit has dedicated none his equal. His passing will be as a light, a beacon that others may follow, a man not ashamed of his adopted race and not forgetful of them and their cause during most of his life.

BE IT THEREFORE RESOLVED, that we, the members of the Akwesasne Six Nations Indian Museum, extend our sincere sympathy to the sorrowing bereaved nearest him and his kin, that we deplore their great loss and while they mourn their loss they mourn the loss of us as a race, the Red Race of America.

BE IT ALSO RESOLVED, that a copy of this resolution be presented to the family of the deceased, our Brother Brave Wolf; a copy framed and placed on the wall of the Six Nations Indian Museum for Indian people and non-Indian people to see, in memory and honour of our great Friend and Brother - Brave Wolf.

Kahionhes
Tehanetorens

New Book on Korczak's Sitting Bull Memorial Relates His Philosophy of Art and Sculpture

Korczak in 1953 with his nearly seven-ton portrait of Sitting Bull. © KORCZAK, Sc.

In honor of Korczak's 76th birth date, Sept. 6, 1984, was the official date of publication at Crazy Horse Memorial of **The Saga of Sitting Bull's Bones** by Robb DeWall. It tells the unusual story behind Sculptor Korczak Ziolkowski's memorial to Sitting Bull and traces the 1953 interstate furor that erupted after Sitting Bull's bones were taken from North Dakota and reburied near Mobridge, S.D., where the memorial is located.*

Mrs. Korczak Ziolkowski highly recommends the book, saying, "Not only does it tell for the first time the full and very interesting story of the 1953 Sitting Bull bones controversy, it presents several sides of Korczak not seen in print previously—especially those sections dealing with his philosophy of art and sculpture."

*The Saga of Sitting Bull's Bones** by Robb DeWall is a 320-page hardback written in the form of a novel, and it contains more than 50 historic photographs as well as reprints of many newspaper articles about the 1953 incident. The book is available exclusively at Crazy Horse Memorial or by mail order (please see page 2).

The Future of Crazy Horse

UNIVERSITY

INDIAN MUSEUM

AVENUE OF
THE CHIEFS

PRESENT STUDIO HOME
AND INDIAN MUSEUM

MEDICAL TRAINING CENTER

© KORCZAK, Sc.

Korczak's detailed, long-range plans for Crazy Horse are illustrated in this painting showing how his non-profit humanitarian project will look in the future when its major goals are accomplished. Those goals are: (1) the mountain carving, (2) the Indian Museum of North America, and (3) the University and Medical Training Center for the North American Indian. Stone portraits of famous American Indian Chiefs will line the Avenue of the Chiefs leading through the University-Medical Training Center complex to the 350-foot-in-diameter Indian Museum near the base of the Crazy Horse sculpture in the round.

Korczak's Presence Will Be There

(Editor's note: The following is an editorial which appeared in the *Watertown* (S.D.) *Public Opinion* on September 12, 1984.)

HAVE YOU EVER BEEN in a room and felt the presence of someone who has been dead, say, a couple of years? Have you ever had to change your mind about something or someone, especially after they were gone? Have you ever been a non-believer in something and then, in a moment, changed that non-belief into an excitement of a crusader?

These questions were answered with a "yes" last weekend by several of us who attended the annual meeting of the S.D. Associated Press Managing Editors Association in Rapid City, which included a complete tour of Korczak Ziolkowski's Crazy Horse Monument near Custer.

We have probably driven by that place maybe a dozen times—maybe a hundred times—since its start back in 1947. But that isn't any different than what was done by hundreds, perhaps thousands, of other native borns. A large number of us have been cynics, and skeptics. "Crazy Polock," "Defacer of mountains," were a couple of the more printable names given this man of vision by many of these South Dakotans—and others.

AND HAVING BEEN a long-time member of the South Dakota editors' group, it is safe to say there is probably no greater number of these cynics and skeptics in any group than there is among editors. It's the nature of the beast. But those of us who stood on the arm of Crazy Horse, nearly 1,000 feet higher than the nearby George Washington—those of us who stared headlong into what will someday become the face of that personage of Crazy Horse, which will hold the four faces of nearby Mount Rushmore, the cynics, the skeptics, soon melted. The unimpressionable were impressed.

We were there on the day of what would have been his 76th birthday. Ziolkowski died unexpectedly on Oct. 20, 1982. But he was still there. His passion, his dedication, to his mountain has been transferred to his most charming and gracious wife, Ruth, and to their children.

The project continues, even though he has been gone these two years. As our doubts fled, one question stood out. How could this passion, this dedication, to this mountainous project be passed on the way it has?

HIS SON, CASIMIR, answered before we had a chance to put it into words. "We have always been a part of it. Dad made it that way. He was that kind of a man." There was deep meaning in his voice. We understood. Korczak said several years ago, "Every man has his mountain—I'm carving mine."

There were decades of debt, and doubt, but the tourists began to come. This continues to finance this giant's dream. This dream is now being transferred to others. It was given to us—the cynics and skeptics—that day on the mountain. His dream will stay. Those cynics and skeptics are fading away.

His dream should be the dream of all South Dakotans. We should be proud that in our state will be two such monuments, when entire nations have none.

BACK IN 1975, Bob Woessner of the *Green Bay Press Gazette* described this giant of a man: "The man is like his name. Powerful, craggy, indecipherable . . . But sound out his name carefully. Core-chock Jewel-kuff-ski. The man is like his name. Poetic, rhythmical, lilting, filled with subtle nuances. Korczak Ziolkowski. Stevedore's shoulders, poet's voice. Mule skinner's tongue, artist's hands . . ."

And as we visited the museum, as Mrs. Ziolkowski described her husband's life, an unfamiliar tourist asked, "Did you know this man personally?"

She said graciously, "I was married to him, but no one really knew all of him."

HIS DREAM WILL go on. His presence will always be there. Perhaps that is why he said, "When the legends die, the dreams end; when the dreams end, there is no more greatness."

His greatness today is Crazy Horse. His greatness is South Dakota. We owe this man, this family, that his dream will someday come true . . .